CHARACTERISTICS OF GOD

A Study of Genesis and Exodus

by

M. Gail Hill and Valerie E. Burton

An Adult Christian Education Curriculum

Parson's Porch Books
www.parsonsporchbooks.com

Characteristics of God: A Study of Genesis and Exodus

ISBN: Softcover 978-1-949888-79-9

Copyright © 2019 by M. Gail Hill and Valerie E. Burton

All rights reserved. No part of this book may be reproduced or transmitted in any form or by any means, electronic or mechanical, including photocopying, recording, or by any information storage and retrieval system, without permission in writing from the publisher.

The scripture quotations contained herein are from the New Revised Standard Version Bible, copyright © 1989, Division of Christian Education of the National Council of Churches of Christ in the U.S.A. Used by permission. All rights reserved.

CHARACTERISTICS OF GOD

A Study of Genesis and Exodus

TABLE OF CONTENTS

Chapter	Page
Introduction	iv

Chapter 1: The God of Creation
   Table 1: Characteristics of God Found in the Creation Stories..................1
   Leader's Guide to Chapter 1..................12

Chapter 2: Judgment: Banishment and Murder
   Table 2: Characteristics of God Found in an Ancient Family Story..................18
   Leader's Guide to Chapter 2..................27

Chapter 3: Judgment: A Flood, a Tower, Two Cities
   Table 3: Characteristics of God Found in Stories of Judgment..................33
   Leader's Guide to Chapter 3..................42

Chapter 4: The Covenant People
   Table 4: Characteristics of God Found in His Promises..................46
   Leader's Guide to Chapter 4..................56

Chapter 5: Problems with a Curse, a Timeline, and a Coat
   Table 5: Characteristics of God Found in the Lives of Ancient People..................63
   Leader's Guide to Chapter 5..................71

Chapter 6: Moses and Miracles
   Table 6: Characteristics of God Found in the Moses Story..................75
   Leader's Guide to Chapter 6..................84

Chapter 7: Plagues and Delivery
   Table 7: Characteristics of God Identified During the Plague Period..................87
   Leader's Guide to Chapter 7..................98

Chapter 8: Miracles in the Wilderness
   Table 8: Characteristics of God Found in the Wilderness Experience..................102
   Leader's Guide to Chapter 8..................112

Chapter 9: Fire and Clouds
   Table 9: Characteristics of God Found in Signs of His Presence..................116
   Leader's Guide to Chapter 9..................123

Chapter 10: The Commandments
   Table 10: Characteristics of God Shown in the Ten Commandments..................128
   Leader's Guide to Chapter 10..................141

Appendix One: Who Wrote the First Five Books..................149

INTRODUCTION

GOALS OF THE STUDY

This study is about dialogue, exploration, and strengthening faith. The objective is to have people explore the details of their beliefs and feelings about their personal faith, and its application to modern life. The hope is that all participants will grow in understanding and adoration of God.

PRELIMINARY THOUGHTS

The desire to know more about the being we call "God" is a common human characteristic. This desire is true within all the world's major religions and is often true about those people who think of themselves as non-religious as well. There is something deeply intriguing about the possibility of an entity supremely more powerful than ourselves. And there is something even more amazing and absolutely astonishing about this same being who loves us and calls us by name (Isaiah 43:1).

In Christianity—especially Protestantism—there is a historical predilection to study Jesus rather than to focus on God, called Abba by Jesus; it is not that God is ignored, but rather that we as humans have an easier time relating to the One who lived and walked among us. Pinnock and Brown asked:

> What is God like? How shall we speak of God who is both near us and yet who transcends the whole world? Although the Bible does not present a systematic doctrine of God that can be easily reproduced, it provides building blocks for such a doctrine. The Scriptures bear a rich witness to the variegated encounters his people have enjoyed with God in a variety of situations.[1]

We shall study clues in scripture which seem to shed light on the characteristics of God. The Biblical revelation is set within a historical context that relates to our humanity; it is not simply a list of things to believe about God. Since we seek to know about Him, we search the pages of Scripture where we find that God loves us and seeks to relate to us. So, we strive to know God better as a response to that love.

THREE BASIC ASSUMPTIONS FOR THIS STUDY

1. **Proceed with Faith**. We begin by assuming that we are faith people and we read the Bible stories seeking the profound truths to be found there. We study Scripture in order to more fully understand the God we worship, to learn how to live, and to affirm our faith. By faith we submit our lives to God. Faith does not mean that we believe in magic, or that we give up the intellect that came from God when we were created in His image. Faith will guide each of us in how best to embrace holy Scripture.

2. **A Humble Approach to Study**. It may seem very presumptuous to dare to "study" the omnipresent God who is actually present with us. Imagine if we were attempting to study a friend who was present in the same room, but to whom we never addressed our questions! In addition, we dare to talk about the Creator as if we actually have the ability to comprehend such a being! We, as humans, can never fully comprehend the Almighty; we can only try to understand what has been voluntarily revealed to us by the Creator—through Scripture, Jesus, and the Holy Spirit. Therefore, humbleness in our prayerful approach to this study is essential.

3. **Word Usage**. Words are important in the literal meaning they convey, and also in the delivery of subtle biases. While we use the common terms of "Old Testament" and "New Testament," we recognize that this may lead some to think the messages in the early Bible no longer have meaning in today's world. In addition, some translations of the Bible use "new testament" to mean the new covenant that Jesus brought into being and spoke of at the Last Supper rather than to mean the collection of books and epistles we think of today as the New Testament.

The second word usage rule we shall follow in these sessions is about gender. Most often we will use the masculine pronouns when discussing God. This is because we are directly studying what Scripture says, and there we find the masculine used. We acknowledge that many people of faith find comfort in seeing God as Mother and we will note the more feminine characteristics of God found in the Torah and in the rest of Scripture as we move through the first two biblical books.

RESPECT FOR ALL VIEWS

We will attempt to respect and be inclusive of all those along the continuum of faith. This means that some passages will be explored from both conservative faith and from liberal faith perspectives. This is not about convincing anyone to change beliefs—what can be finally gleaned from this study is up to the individual reader. By reviewing all perspectives of the issues, we learn from each other—sometimes strengthening our original beliefs and other times encountering significant challenges for personal growth. "Our interpretations reveal less about God or the Bible than they do about ourselves. They reveal what we want to defend, what we want to attack, what we want to ignore, what we're unwilling to question..." [2]

Quotes of Scripture in these sessions are from the New Revised Standard Version (NRSV) because we believe it to be accurate and understandable. However, it may be helpful to some participants to have them read the same passages from their preferred translation.

LIMITATIONS OF THIS STUDY

The endeavor to understand more about God from rereading the entire two testaments of Scripture would require an encyclopedic expository. Instead, these sessions are focused on Genesis and Exodus. Genesis seems the perfect place to start when taking up the difficult and daunting task of discovering more about God the Creator. Many people of faith think of Genesis as being about how everything got started—how the world came to be and how human existence began. Another perspective is that Genesis is about the Creator of it all, or "Who started everything." The rest of the Bible is about God's redemptive work to bring us closer to Him.[3]

We will take the viewpoint that Genesis was never meant to be a book of science describing HOW creation was accomplished, but rather it is about the God who created the cosmos and humanity. However, we will note the findings of science when these are important for understanding Scripture.

SCIENCE AND FAITH

Humankind has benefited greatly from the work of scientists. For example, medical science has given us the ability to prolong life and ease suffering. Medical science benefits from the work of many of the sciences—biology, chemistry, physics, and others. While we are grateful, we do not elevate the sciences to become our gods.

We will review explanations from scientists in the sessions in this book—both those scientists of faith and those who do not believe in a higher power. Some scientific explanations are reasonable—about miracles, for example. In those explanations, we find that God uses the resources of His creation to teach and to help. This does not deny the role of God, but rather shows us how God is present and interacts with the created world. However, there are events in the creation which are beyond the ability of human knowledge to explain. For example, Cham and Whiteson wrote about the atom that if the proton charge did not "...precisely balance the negative charge of the electron...you couldn't form stable neutral atoms. Without those perfect negative 1/3 and positive 2/3 charges, we wouldn't be here. There would be no chemistry, no biology, and no life."[4] Science has not been able to explain just why the charges are this way. However, faith can explain it: God's creation was perfectly done down to the atomic level!

Remember as you explore these sessions, that science has provided explanations for only around five percent of how the universe works; ninety-five percent remains unknown and unexplained.[4] This does not mean that we dismiss the work of scientists. Rather it means that there is much room for faith's role in understanding our existence. Ninety-five percent of the universe in which we live is so mysterious we can only imagine the mighty works of God as He molded and formed the stars and beyond.

GRATITUDE

We owe a great debt to a few wise people who volunteered their services in editing grammar, and who also held us to sound interpretation of Scripture. These are people of faith who live exemplary lives. Any errors the reader may find in this book belong solely to the two authors, and not to these wonderful friends. The editors include Roderick Davis, Joe Dean, Carol Dean, Cindy Goodwin, Paul Hall, Kenneth Hinton, Pat Hudson, Fisher Humphries, Rosalind McClanahan, Morgan Ponder, Peggy Sanderford Ponder, and Don Roberts.

Much gratitude is also owed to a group of volunteers who endured one semester of this study material as we were writing it. These individuals allowed us to test the materials for clarity, interest, and application to modern life situations. The students in the class included Janet Anthony, Bart Grooms, Lynda Grooms, Ralph Hoefelman, David Hoefelman, John Hollis, Ken Hinton, and Peggy Sanderford Ponder.

We hope that all who study with us will re-awaken in themselves an intense desire to know more about God. Read on and enter prayerfully and respectfully into a study to learn more about the God we worship.

REFERENCES

1. Pinnock, C.H., & Brown, D. (1998). *Theological crossfire: An evangelical/liberal dialogue.* Eugene, OR: Wipf and Stock Publishers, p. 63.
2. McLaren, B. (2001). *A new kind of Christian: A tale of two friends on a spiritual journey.* San Francisco: Jossey-Bass, p. 50.
3. Miller, S.M. (2007). *The complete guide to the Bible.* Uhrichsville, Ohio: Barbour Publishing, Inc.
4. Cham, J., & Whiteson, D. (2017). *We have no idea.* New York: Riverhead Books, p. 54.

CHAPTER 1 — THE GOD OF CREATION
GENESIS 1–3a

Table 1: Characteristics of God Found in the Creation Stories

Characteristic	Reference	Characteristics	Reference
Creates Life	Genesis 1:26	Values Names	Isaiah 43:1
Creates Magnificence	Genesis 1: 1–19	Cares about Our Needs	Genesis 2:22–24
Gives Free Will	Genesis 2:16–17 Genesis 3:1–7	Gives Purpose	Genesis 1:26–30 Genesis 2:15 Genesis 2:20b
Rests	Genesis 2:2–3	Recognizes Time	Genesis 1:20–31
Creates and Judges What is Good	Genesis 1	Provides Nourishment	Genesis 1:30

Central Theme of this session: Looking through the lens of ancient civilization's views of the world, we gain perspective about the creator of it all, or about Who started everything.

Central Question of this session: How were the characteristics of God revealed through Creation?

AN OVERVIEW

This chapter begins the study of what the Bible tells us about God and creation. We usually consider the first books of the Bible as a history of the early Jews, but they also provide important glimpses of the Creator and how God relates to creation. The Genesis stories help us to understand ourselves and our relationship to God by exploring the origin of the cosmos and of humanity.

Exercise 1: Before we get into the verse by verse study, what can you share about the characteristics of God from your previous studies in Genesis?

Exercise 2: Have someone read Genesis 1: 1–19 to the group.

<u>God creates magnificence</u>. The characteristics of God presented in these verses tell us about a creative ability unmatched by anything humans can imagine or do; we can speak all we wish, but no new worlds result! God is overwhelmingly powerful and can create wonder out of chaos.

The Genesis creation chapters are quite beautiful when appreciated poetically. There is a poetic rhythm in the way the days and the task for each day are written in the first chapter. Everything is done in an orderly, step-wise fashion; beauty is invited to come out of chaos. Each day a new step is taken and the Creator determines that day's work is "good." The last day's work involves two living beings made in the very image of the Creator. Finally, God rests, thereby putting a period at the end of the poem.

Theologians debate about whether God first set things in motion and then stopped creating, or whether creation continues. The important distinction seems to be whether God created once and stepped away, leaving us alone—a belief from Deism[1], or whether God continues to be involved. We shall see in following verses that God did not leave us alone after creating, but continues to hear the pleas of His people, and to intervene for their wellbeing. Whether or not you think God is still creating, we have evidence in Scripture that we have not been abandoned.

SCIENCE AND FAITH

People of faith may encounter challenges when they compare the biblical creation stories with scientific theories of creation. It sometimes seems as if a devout Christian cannot also be an educated consumer of science. A careful study of historical as well as modern scientists shows that God cannot be ignored by the thinking person; there are many scientists who openly profess belief in the risen Lord. Examples follow of some in the scientific community who either hint at a mysterious power guiding creation, or who openly proclaim the existence of God.

Consider a quote from *A Brief History of Time* by the late Stephen Hawkins—a prominent and popular scientist—that concerns electrical charge and mass ratios of subatomic particles: "The remarkable fact is that the values of these numbers seem to have been very finely adjusted to make possible the development of life."[1] The meaning to the believer is clear; a powerful creator did indeed "finely adjust" the universe so that life could exist. There are other indicators in his book of something working beyond the natural processes. Hawkins did not profess a belief in God even though some of his statements, like that just above, indicate more than scientific objectivity.

For people of faith, there is ample evidence in scientific writing to support biblical principles and God's hand in creation. Walter Isaacson wrote that free will for humans is permitted because of "the math at the core of quantum physics, which describes how events at the subatomic level are governed by statistical probabilities rather than laws that determine things with certainty."[2]

Einstein—assumed by many to be the most intelligent scientist to ever live—had this to say about faith: "As a child I received instruction both in the Bible and in the Talmud. I am a Jew, but I am enthralled by the luminous figure of the Nazarene." When asked if he accepted the historical existence of Jesus, he said, "Unquestionably! No one can read the Gospels without feeling the actual presence of Jesus. His personality pulsates in every word. No myth is filled with such life."[3] Einstein did not affirm a faith in Jesus as the Son of God, nor did he have faith in a personal God, but he was able to see beyond the physics and the formulas to know that something mysterious existed outside of our ability to explain.

The origins of science come from within the Church itself. Priests in the Church had the time to wonder about events happening around them, and to begin the exploration of nature. The first universities in Europe were founded by the Catholic Church during the Middle Ages.[4]

There have been and continue to be many scientists who profess belief in God. Charles Townes (1915–2015), who won the Nobel Prize in Physics, is the author of *The Convergence of Science and Religion*.[5] A name more familiar to the lay person is Wernher von Braun (1912–1977) who contributed substantially to the development of space exploration. "As an adult, he developed a firm belief in the Lord and in the afterlife. He was pleased to have opportunities to speak to peers (and anybody else who would listen) about his faith and biblical beliefs."[6]

Francis Collins is a physician-geneticist who led the Human Genome Project and served as Director of the National Human Genome Research Institute before becoming Director of the National Institutes of Health; he is also a Christian. He wrote *The Language of God: A Scientist Presents Evidence for Belief.* He professes God as the creator who set forth the events leading to life on earth.[7]

God creates and judges what is good. God did not just create randomly; He created "good." Each time something new was formed, he judged it to be good. We worship the One who speaks good things into being.

Exercise 3: Name some things in our world which you would label "good."

Exercise 4: Read Genesis 2:18–20 and look for something that is "not good."

NAMES ARE IMPORTANT

God names. Isaiah 43:1 says, that because we belong to God, He knows our names and even calls us by our names. The names of things and people seem important to God. After God created the animals, He brought them to the man for naming. Later in Genesis we will study the name changes of Abraham and Sarah once they came to know God. In the New Testament, there is the example of Saul becoming Paul following his conversion.

Names are also important to humans. Parents put a lot of thought into the naming of children. But scientists do not name the laboratory animals that they will eventually sacrifice in their research, and hunters do not name the deer they kill. We do give names to the animals who are our companions—our dogs, cats, horses, and birds. Giving a name somehow conveys gravitas and implies relationship.

Exercise 5: Share with the group any significance in your name or in your family names. Are you named for someone special? How has your own name, given by your parents, affected your life?

At this point let us consider the names of God. It was Sarah's poor Egyptian slave, Hagar, who first called God by name (Genesis 16:13); before her, God was addressed by titles such as "Lord." Jesus called God "Father" and taught us to pray using that term of address. But that is not the only name in the Bible for God. Perhaps the most mysterious name was provided by God to Moses: "I AM WHO I AM" (Exodus 3:14-15). This Exodus chapter goes on to say, "Thus you shall say to Israelites, 'I AM has sent me to you.'"

Jehovah is one of the seven names of God that were given special significance by medieval Jewish tradition. The seven sacred names include the tetragrammation YHWH (pronounced Yahweh), El, Elohim, Eloah, Elohai, El Shaddai, and Tzevaot.[8] Ruth 2:4 indicates the name Yahweh was being pronounced out loud during the fifth century BCE even though by the third century BCE the name was not to be spoken aloud by any but the High Priest and then only in the Holy of Holies.[9] This prohibition seems to have come from the fear of taking the Lord's name in vain.

After the Temple was destroyed in 70 CE there was no Holy of Holies in which to pronounce the name of God. In modern times, YHWH is not pronounced by most religious Jews. Rather the name *Adonai* is used at specific times and the name *HaShem* at other times. The surviving Greek texts use either *Kyrois* or *Theos*.

GOD AS MOTHER

At no time is a definite feminine name used in Genesis and Exodus, the books we are studying. Since the biblical books, poems, songs, and letters were written by men in an ancient time, this is not surprising. During the ages in which the biblical writings arose, women were not formally educated and were mostly illiterate. Knowing this, we would not expect to find the female perspective widely represented.

The use of motherly titles is not prohibited in Scripture. Many today are comforted with the idea that there is a motherly aspect to the God of creation. After all, both male and female were created in God's image. There are several references to very motherly behaviors, and there are biblical passages indicating that God is also "Mother." In Hosea 11:3–4, we are told that God taught Ephraim to walk, and "I took them up in my arms...I was to them like those who lift infants to their cheeks. I bent down to them and fed them." In Isaiah 42:14, God is described as a woman in labor. There are other references to motherly behaviors by God which will be explored in other chapters. Perhaps it is time for "Heavenly Mother" or some similar address to become part of our worship.

Exercise 6: Share in the group what you think about the use of feminine names for God. Does this idea comfort you or make you uncomfortable?

THE CONCEPT OF TIME

<u>God recognizes time</u>. Evening and morning came and went. We do not know if the concept of "day and night" for the omnipresent God is the same 24 hours that we use. If God could simply speak a world into existence, He could certainly do it in a 24-hour time frame, or even in a milli-second. But the God who is both the Alpha and the Omega could view time very differently than we who are limited by the rotation of our planet between light and dark. In Genesis 2:4 we find there were "generations" involved in the creation of heaven and earth.

We experience a dissonance between our sense of time and God's perspective every time we pray specifically. Answers to our prayers seldom occur minutes after the prayer; sometimes years go by before we are aware that God has responded. It is often in retrospect that we see where God has been in our lives.

Time has been a somewhat fluid concept in the history of human understanding. Both Roman and Chinese ancient calendars described ten months in a year. The early Greeks only numbered their months instead of naming them, since the month was determined by the lunar year of 354 days. The calendar we use today is the Gregorian calendar introduced in 1582,[10] many centuries after the creation accounts were written.

Perhaps the scribes of the Genesis parchments imposed their own familiar concepts of time in order to convey an understandable measure of God's time. Or, a 24-hour span may have been exactly what occurred between each "day" of creation.

An interesting aside is what science tells us about time: Einstein's theory of relativity posits that there is no unique absolute "time" even for humans.[11] What we can say with assurance is, regardless of the time factor, creation proceeded according to God's intentional design and according to God's timing.

Exercise 7: How do you value time? Do you have any sense of urgency about the passage of time?

Exercise 8: Have someone in the group read Genesis 1:20–31.

LIFE CREATION

God creates life. God's awesome power is manifested wonderfully for us through the creation of life. God can create life, can take it away, and, as with his Son, can conquer death and resurrect to new life. In Genesis chapter one, an order of life creation is given: first plants; then fish, birds, and other creatures; and, finally, humans. Both male and female humans were created at the same time in this passage, and both were created in the image of God.

Exercise 9: Given that males and females were both created in the image of God and at the same time, what does this say about God's view of males and females? How should the Church actualize the creation of both sexes in God's image?

The question arises as to why God would create humans at all. Was it about loneliness? He did not seem to be alone since he spoke of letting "...us make humankind in our image, according to our likeness" (Genesis 1:26). The New Testament records that God was not alone in John chapter one.

Did God desire companions similar to our pets? If that were the case, creation activity could have stopped after the creatures of the planet were created. Instead, God created male and female in His own image and gave them the ability to consider their actions, to have free will, and to make choices of consequence.

An astonishing idea: Perhaps God created humans to be recipients of His love! The evidence for this is found throughout the Bible, but most vividly is found in the incarnate Son sent to redeem us. God sent His Son into the world, the world condemned the Son and killed him, and then God sent Jesus back to us after resurrection. Who would do that without an extraordinary amount of love for the ones to be saved.[12]

Exercise 10: Have someone in the group read the second chapter of Genesis.

In this second Genesis chapter, there is a slightly different order of creation. Nothing was growing when man alone was formed from the dust of the ground. Only after man was created did God plant a garden with three kinds of trees—those from which to eat, a tree of life, and a tree of the knowledge of good and evil. And only after God saw that the human male was lonely, were the living creatures formed out of the same dust of the earth.

Darwin's *Theory of Evolution* makes a case for humans having common ancestors with primates. This theory could easily follow from the order of creation in the first chapter, but not from the second chapter of Genesis where the man is created first before any of the animals. Before we get too puffed up, it is important to note in chapter two, that the male was created from dirt! Humbleness is an attribute that God likes (Micah 6:8), and this source of human life ties us to the humblest of earthy beginnings!

Another important reminder for our study of creation is that science and faith are two different things. Science draws conclusions from objective observation, and the author(s) of Genesis were not there at the moments of creation to observe. Faith provides us with explanations for those things which cannot or could not be observed objectively. However, both disciplines search for truth, and both contribute to the understanding of how we experience our lives.

Exercise 11: Why do you suppose there are two versions of creation with substantial differences? How does your faith respond to these differences?

WOMAN AS HELP MEET

God cares about our needs. God saw that the male was alone and it was not good to be alone. Relationships are important to God and to humans: we have already seen that God was not alone at the beginning of creation. Furthermore, God understands our needs and provides for them.

A more detailed description of how the companion, woman, was created is provided in chapter two than what we found for the creation of either sex in chapter one: The man was formed from the dust of the ground and God breathed the breath of life into him. The woman's creation followed. A surgical procedure was performed on the man including anesthesia, removal of a rib, and closure of the wound. The female was created when God recognized loneliness in the man.

The common way in which the term "help meet"—King James Version (KJV)— is interpreted means that Eve, unlike the other beasts of the earth, was to be Adam's helper and companion on the earth. While there are some good things about this KJV interpretation, it doesn't do full justice to what the term "help meet" really means. The original Hebrew term, *ezer*, means something much more profound and powerful than just a helper. Understanding of what God was really saying to Adam allows Eve's true role, and the role of women in God's creation, to be seen much differently. In the NRSV translation of the Bible, we have, "…I will make him a helper as his partner."

Beverly Campbell explained, "According to biblical scholar David Freedman, the Hebrew word translated into English as "help" is *ezer*. This word is a combination of two roots, one meaning "to rescue," "to save," and the other meaning "to be strong."[13] Diana Webb wrote that the word *ezer* is found multiple times in the Hebrew Bible; the meaning of the word is "savior" in eight of those occurrences. At other times the word is used to mean "strength" and is even used "to describe how God is an *ezer* to man."[13] Psalm 70:5 and 121:2 also use the word *ezer* to refer to God's help. The use of *ezer* in references to both Eve and God helps us understand that God does have a feminine component as well as the masculine. In Hebrew, the word *ezer* means that the one providing help has the necessary power or ability to help; power is part of the translation.

Beverly Campbell wrote "Suppose we had all, male and female alike, been taught to understand Genesis 2:18 as something like the following, 'It is not good that man should be alone. I will make him a companion of strength and power who has a saving power and is equal with him."[13]

Exercise 12: From what does Eve save Adam?

Exercise 13: Have someone in the group read Galatians 3:26–29. What do these verses tell us about the characteristics of God?

Exercise 14: Does this material change how you think of yourself if you are a woman, or how you think of your wife, mother, sister, daughter if you are a man?

The purpose of these sessions is not to push for gender equality, but to learn more about who the Creator God is and how best to worship and honor God. With that in mind, we may conclude that men and women are spiritually equal in God's sight but have different physical roles in earthly existence. **The amazing fact is that the most powerful entity in existence loves and seeks relationship with us as individuals.**

Exercise 15: How do you practice relationship with other humans in your life? How are these the same or different in the ways you relate to God?

Exercise 16: Can you think of an example that Jesus gave on how best to relate to him? If not, read Matthew 25:35–40.

SOURCES OF KNOWLEDGE ABOUT GOD

As we study the original revelation provided in the Bible, we shall see that God has reached out to us throughout history; He continues to do so today. First, we were provided with ancient texts about creation and the early people with whom God revealed His existence. Later, God became incarnate and lived among us as Jesus, and followed that by sending the Holy Spirit. If the Bible alone were totally sufficient as a book of instructions on how to live, there would have been no need for Jesus to die at Calvary, nor for the Holy Spirit to provide guidance. We were created to need actual relationship with God; the Bible provides the guide to that relationship. The example Jesus provided for us in the New Testament gives weight to this view. Jesus, in his relationship with others, took care of healing and food provision on the Sabbath when needed, regardless of what the Old Testament said about the Sabbath. He knew that charity was more important than the written law.

HUMANITY'S PURPOSE

God gives purpose. Immediately after creating humankind, God gave them some very big tasks—to rule all the animal kingdom, to increase and fill the earth, and to subdue the earth (Genesis 1: 26–30). Maybe this giving of tasks is what we mean when we say we are "called" to a mission. In Genesis chapter two, man's purpose is not power over other creatures, but his purpose is to till the garden of Eden and care for it (Genesis 2:15). Woman's purpose is to be a strong partner (Genesis 2:20b).

Exercise 17: Have you experienced a call to do something special in your life? Share with the group what this concept has meant to you.

Exercise 18: What does it mean "to subdue the earth?"

God provides for our physical nourishment. Genesis 1:30 says that humans and animals are given plants for food. The first two humans were vegetarians! It is only after sin had come into the world and after the flood, that humans are told they can eat flesh (Genesis 9:3). In Daniel 1:11–20, Daniel and colleagues were given only vegetables to eat and appeared healthier after several days than those people eating meat. The choice to be vegetarian is not without precedent in the Christian faith: Many early church fathers were vegetarians, including St. Basil, St. John Chrysostom, and St. Francis of Assisi.

Romans 14:1–23, however, provides a way of looking at both sides of diet—eating meat is okay and so is eating only vegetables; we are not to judge. Matthew 15:11 notes that it is not what we put in our mouths that causes us to sin, but rather it is those harmful words that come out of our mouths.

The more important concept is how we treat the animals we use for food. In today's world, meat production has become a matter of maximizing "protein units per square foot" of factory farm space. What a cold-hearted concept! Nonhuman animals belong to God—their Creator—and not to us. God gave us responsibility for them and we should honor His trust. "We should be the people, because we're formed and shaped by the Bible, who call the consciences of those around us to care about responsible treatment of animals."[14]

Exercise 19: Where do you stand on the dietary issue? Are dietary restrictions of any kind part of your faith practice? What about fasting?

Exercise 20: Have someone in the group who lives with a companion animal share what, if anything, the animal contributes to human quality of life.

God Rests. On the seventh day creation was completed and God ceased from work. The Bible says that God "rested." It is difficult to think of the omnipresent, omnipotent, and omniscient God as needing rest, so it may be that God simply ceased work. Or perhaps God considers that rest is another "good" thing and has modeled that for us. Whatever the answer, this is part of the pattern of creation, and seems to be important.

Exercise 21: One of the ten commandments requires us to keep a holy day out of the seven days. Does this provision for a day of devotion to God coincide with a need for rest? Does it mirror God's need since we are made in His image? Do you rest on Sundays or treat it like any other day?

Exercise 22: Have someone in the group read the third chapter of Genesis.

<u>God gives us free will</u>. In Genesis 3:1–7, the humans were tempted to disobey the one rule God gave them. They didn't have 10 commandments or the 3 behavior rules in Micah 6 verses, nor did they have the 2 greatest commandments (Matthew 22:36–40); they only had one rule, and they made the decision to disobey it. But this discussion is not about what humans have done; it is about who God is. He created us and gave us the ability to make choices. He could have made us His puppets, but did not. As much as the most powerful entity in all of existence could have controlled us, God did not impose His will on us.

Exercise 23: In exercise one you were asked to share what you believed about the characteristics of God. Now that you've studied the creation chapters more closely, have any of your ideas about God changed?

CONCLUSION

We have come to the end of the Genesis creation chapters. Regardless of how we as individuals view these accounts—literally or as sacred stories given to convey profound truth, we know some very reassuring things about God: He creates, prefers goodness in the cosmos, provides for our needs, and cares about us. These are very comforting things to know about God. In the following sessions, we will examine the judgments of God. We will examine our understanding of the judgment of the Eden occupants, of the first murderer, of the builders of a tower, of two cities filled with evil deeds, and of all of humanity in the flood story.

REFERENCES

1. Hawking, S. (1988). *A brief history of time.* New York: Bantam Books Trade Paperbacks, p. 129.
2. Isaacson, W. (2014). *The innovators.* New York: Simon & Schuster, p. 42.
3. Isaacson, W. (2007 April 5). Einstein and the mind of God. *Time*, 169, p. 47. Retrieved from https://www.onfaith.co/onfaith/2007/04/27/einstein-and-the-mind-of-god/3763.

4. Woods, T.E., Jr. (2005). The Catholic Church and the creation of the university. Retrieved from http://www.catholiceducation.org/en/education/catholic-contributions/the-catholic-church-and-the-creation-of-the-university.html.
5. Towns, C. (1966). *The convergence of science and religion.* Armock, New York: IBM. Vol. 32,2, p.2-7. Retrieved from http://www.templetonprize.org/pdfs/THINK.pdf.
6. _____. (2014). The religious affiliation of rocket engineer and inventor Wernher von Braun. *Adherents.com.* Retrieved from http://www.adherents.com/people/pv/Wernher_von_Braun.html.
7. Collins, F. (2006). *Collins: Why this scientist believes in God.* Retrieved from (http://www.cnn.com/2007/US/04/03/collins.commentary/index.html.
8. _____. (1965). Names of God in Judaism. In *The reader's encyclopedia* (2nd ed.) Retrieved from http://www.newworldencyclopedia.org/entry/Names_of_God_in_Judaism.
9. Harris, S.L. (1985). *Understanding the Bible: A reader's introduction,* (2nd ed.), p. 21. Palo Alto, CA: Mayfield.
10. _____. (n.d.). History of Calendars. *Wikipedia.* Retrieved from (https://en.wikipedia.org/wiki/History_of_calendars.
11. Hawkins, S. (1998), p.147.
12. Note: John Claypool was the pastor at Broadway Baptist Church (1971-1976) when one of the authors was a member there and heard him preach this sermon.
13. _____. (2010 Nov 9). The real meaning of the term "help meet." *Women in the Scriptures.* Retrieved from http://www.womeninthe scriptures.com/2010/11/real-meaning-or-term-help-meet.html.
14. Camosy, C. (2017, January 6). *Birmingham News,* p. A11.

CHAPTER 1   LEADERS GUIDE: THE GOD OF CREATION
GENESIS 1-3a

PRELIMINARY THOUGHTS

The leader's guide can be used to help you move the discussion forward in a thoughtful, non-judgmental manner. This study is not about convincing anyone to change beliefs about ancient writings; it is about dialogue, exploration, and strengthening faith. The objective is to have people explore the details of their personal faith. The hope is that all participants will grow in understanding of God.

This first chapter is designed to last for at least two discussion periods if not more. You may encounter some disagreement in this session within the group. For example, some life-long Christians have never considered that there are significant differences in the two creation versions. Work to maintain a courteous environment which allows every participant to feel safe in expressing beliefs.

AN OVERVIEW

Exercise 1: Before we get into the verse by verse study, what can you share about the characteristics of God from your previous studies in Genesis?

Ask how they came to believe certain things about God. Was it through Sunday School, childhood songs, sermons? List answers on the board so you can compare later in the session to any new insights.

Exercise 2: Have someone read Genesis 1:1–19 to the group.

After the group reads through this section about Deism, ask them if God is still creating. People will probably say newborns are new creations. Or beauty such as sunsets are created new daily. Do not argue because this is not an article of faith; salvation does not depend on belief about this question. Furthermore, it may be true that God's creative hand is uniquely new in each person or each expression of nature's beauty.

SCIENCE AND FAITH

Exercise 3: Name some things in our world which you would label "good."

Remind them that God called all of His creation "good," but wait before saying this until the group has considered and discussed. A more prolonged and in-depth discussion might be: how did evil get into the world if God's creation was all good? This approach can explore even the creation of bacteria and viruses which cause disease. Some say malaria was a good thing when it kept humans out of the jungles and, therefore, from destroying the rain forests.[1] There is also research indicating that sickle cell trait conveys some resistance to the malaria parasite because of the sickle cell shape of the blood cell.[2] So perhaps <u>everything</u> originally had some "good."

Exercise 4: Read Genesis 2: 18–20 and look for something that is "not good."

The answer is that man being alone was not good. God then created woman.

NAMES ARE IMPORTANT

Exercise 5: Share with the group any significance in your name or in your family names. Are you named for someone special? How has your own name, given by your parents, affected your life?

Do you name your pets? Your chickens, cows, horses? What is the difference between those creatures you name and those you do not name? Do you think new Christians should have a name change similar to what happened with Abram/Abraham and Sarai/Sarah? What if a missionary leads a Hindu in India or a Muslim in the Middle East to become a Christian? Should that new Christian be required to change his/her name to a more biblical-sounding name? A name change would make sure the person stood out in the cultural context. Is that good? Remind them that salvation depends only on one thing: acceptance of Jesus as Lord and Saviour.

GOD AS MOTHER

Exercise 6: Share in the group what you think about the use of feminine names for God. Does this idea comfort you or make you uncomfortable?

Listen carefully to any differences between the opinions of women and of men in your class. Ask them if they notice any significant difference of opinion between the genders. If anyone strongly objects to a feminine aspect of God, have them explore that a little more, but without putting pressure on them to change. For example, you might ask if they have a negative impression of motherhood. Or ask if a feminine name makes God seem weak. Be sensitive as to how you handle this.

THE CONCEPT OF TIME

Exercise 7: How do you value time? Do you have any sense of urgency about the passage of time?

The poem *If* by Kipling has this line:
**"If you can fill the unforgiving minute
With sixty seconds worth of distance run,**
Yours is the earth and all that's in it
And—which is more—you'll be a man, my son!"

Ask if their lives are governed by the need to be productive every minute. Ask how they value "down time"—naps, or just sitting and watching grass grow. How is their attitude about use of time influenced by life goals?

How has the age of social media and smart phones had an impact on their time?

Exercise 8: Have someone in the group read Genesis 1: 20–31.

LIFE CREATION

Exercise 9: Given that males and females were both created in the image of God and at the same time, what does this say about God's view of males and females? How should the Church actualize the creation of both sexes in God's image?

Ask if they've ever experienced worship led by a woman. Ask how we can justify not allowing women to be preachers if they believe both men and women were created in God's image. Do not argue about this, but allow the pendulum of opinion to swing.

Exercise 10: Have someone in the group read the second chapter of Genesis.

Exercise 11: Why do you suppose there are two versions of creation with substantial differences? How does your faith respond to these differences?

Does a different version of a(any) Scripture challenge your faith? Does it matter that the Gospels have slight variations in the telling of the life of Jesus? The biblical manuscripts were written by humans inspired by God. Does God allow for individual differences in expression?

WOMAN AS HELP MEET

Exercise 12: From what does Eve save Adam?

She saves him from loneliness in the garden. Some might argue that later she "unsaves" him by getting him to eat from the forbidden tree. How does modern woman "save" her partner?

Exercise 13: Have someone in the group read Galatians 3:26–29. What do these verses tell us about the characteristics of God?

It seems to mean that God is no respecter of differences among persons. We all are His children, and heirs of the Kingdom. Ask how these verses influence one's daily life.

Exercise 14: Does this material change how you think of yourself if you are a woman, or how you think of your wife, mother, sister, daughter if you are a man?

Be prepared for someone to say one parent was abusive so it is difficult to think of God as that gender. Do not try to do pastoral counseling with this person during the session time, but be sensitive to your availability following the class. Others in the class may try to "help" the person expressing this experience. You may need to redirect the conversation to protect both participants. You as teacher might find it helpful to have a list of qualified counselors.

The next two exercises (15 and 16) can be discussed together or separately.

Exercise 15: How do you practice relationship with other humans in your life? How are these the same or different in the ways you relate to God?

This discussion may elicit strong emotions about fairness, reciprocal love, resentment, or blame placed on the other person. Allow space for the emotions to flow. Don't be afraid to let moments of silence be part of the class experience.

Exercise 16: Can you think of an example that Jesus gave on how best to relate to him? If not, read Matthew 25:35–40.

Remember that the session at this point is discussing gender matters. Redirect if need be so that the class is considering how to relate to the opposite sex in a way that Christ would say, "you did that for me."

SOURCES OF KNOWLEDGE ABOUT GOD

HUMANITY'S PURPOSE

Exercise 17: Have you experienced a call to do something in your life? Share with the group what this concept has meant to you.

Does a call have to be to full-time Christian ministry? Could it be to any life's work such as medicine or construction? Suppose I really desire to be an artist—could that be a calling from God? Have them read Exodus 31:1-3 before completing the discussion of exercise 17.

Exercise 18: What does it mean "to subdue the earth?"

Discuss what this involves. Does it mean that anything humans do to the Earth is sanctioned by God? Does it make it OK to destroy the rain forests? Does it mean you should make the best use of your own small plot of ground? Would the time the Scriptures were written make a difference if written during the era of settled farming instead of during nomadic wanderings?

Exercise 19: Where do you stand on the dietary issue? Are dietary restrictions of any kind part of your faith practice? What about fasting?

Let the class discuss as much or as little as they please. If there are vegetarians in the group, ask them what led them to the dietary practice. Ask how people with any special dietary needs—by choice or due to health issues (diabetes or low salt requirements, as examples)—handle this when they are a guest in another's home.

Exercise 20: Have someone in the group who lives with a companion animal share what, if anything, the animal contributes to human quality of life.

There are people who treat their companion animals like members of their family. Consider if the class members have thought to send condolence cards to any church members who have lost a companion animal. Emphasize that people should never tell horrific animal abuse stories in a group without knowing ahead of time that this is OK; some people have chronic nightmares after hearing these kinds of stories.

People who have not experienced the companionship of a pet sometimes believe others use pets to cover loneliness. This idea is hurtful to those who love their pets. It essentially means, "If something weren't wrong with you, you would have a human companion instead of needing animals to fill the void." This could possibly be true for some, but is not a blanket conclusion. People have sensibilities to different things; some devote themselves so extensively to art or to ambition that their personal relationships are disasters. So, whom would you worry about most: the person with multiple failed marriages, or the single person who lives with companion animals?

Exercise 21: One of the ten commandments requires us to keep a holy day out of the seven days. Does this provision for a day of devotion to God coincide with a need for rest? Does it mirror God's need since we are made in His image? Do you rest on Sundays or treat it like any other day?

Some people's jobs are indispensable to the lives of the rest of us—nurses, doctors, electricians, plumbers, and many others. Ask if anyone in the class has neighbors who do this Sunday work and if they might thank them for continuing to work when others get freer weekends. Consider the restaurant workers who serve your Sunday lunch—maybe an extra gratuity amount would be in order. If you are one of those indispensable workers, consider exchanging shifts with a person you work with who is of another faith on their sacred days.

This issue will be revisited during the discussion of the ten commandments.

Exercise 22: Have someone in the group read the third chapter of Genesis.

Exercise 23: In exercise one you were asked to share what you believed about the characteristics of God. Now that you've studied the creation chapters more closely, have any of your ideas about God changed?

The class leader may want to bring the original list back to the class and compare any changes or additions.

Revisit the central theme and question.

Central Theme of this lesson: Looking through the lens of ancient civilization's views of the world, we gain perspective about the creator of it all, or about Who started everything.

Central Question of this lesson: How were the characteristics of God revealed through Creation?

REFERENCES

1. Nuwer, R. (May 23, 2013). *Save the Amazon, increase malaria*. Smithsonian.com. Retrieved from https://www.smithsonianmag.com/science-nature/save-the-amazon-increase-malaria-78485425/.
2. Aidoo, M., Terlouw, D.J., Kolczak, M.S., McElroy, P.D., ter Kuile, F.O., Kariuki, S., Nahlen, B.L., Lal, A.A., & Udhayakumar, V. (2002). Protective effects of the sickle cell gene against malaria morbidity and mortality. *Lancet*, 359:1311-1312.

CHAPTER 2   JUDGMENT—BANISHMENT AND MURDER
GENESIS 3–4

Table 2: Characteristics of God Found in an Ancient Family Story

Characteristic	Reference	Characteristic	Reference
Seeks us	Genesis 3:6–19	Speaks to us	Genesis 3:6–19
Tempts us	Genesis 3:6–19 Matthew 4:1	Judges	Genesis 3:4–19 Genesis 4:7
Is merciful	Genesis 4:13–16	Listens and hears us	Genesis 3:13
Forgives and restores	Revelation 22:2	Allows us to be tempted	Genesis 3:6–19 Matthew 4:1
Appears in forms that meet our needs	Genesis 3:6–19	Examines motivations as well as deeds	I John 3:12

Central Theme of this lesson: God tempers judgment of humanity with mercy.

Central Question of this lesson: How does God respond to disobedient humanity?

PRELIMINARY THOUGHTS

There is no one unchanging idea contained in the word "god." The word invokes a wide spectrum of meanings, some of which are contradictory or even mutually exclusive. For example, Christians believe in a merciful God largely because of the work of Jesus Christ to redeem creation. But we also have the book of Job in which God appears to make a deal with the devil to bring havoc to Job's life. We should not expect to ever fully understand the Creator, and that is why trust is required.

This chapter and the one that follows are about the judgments God made when people sinned. The theologian C.H. Pinnock wrote that God is aware of and "identifies with the sufferings of people."[1] Pinnock teaches that God does not keep His anger against us forever; God embraces sinners, such as King David in the First Testament, all the while abhorring the sin. These are words of great hope since none of us are perfect as much as we might strive to be. We can know that God understands the nature of those He has created and that His judgments will be just.

There is a cyclical relationship between God and the chosen Hebrew people involving judgment described in the Old Testament. First, the Hebrews are chosen, then they break God's laws, followed by God forgiving them and renewing the Covenant. The message is that God always has a view to restoration of relationship.

THE FIRST DISOBEDIENCE

Exercise 1: Have someone in the group read Genesis 3:6–24.

God seeks us and speaks to us. Genesis 3 tells the story of the first human disobedience to God. It is a very important chapter in the Bible since it tells us how we came to be in such a state of distance from God.

In these passages, the humans eat of the fruit of the tree of knowledge of good and evil. "Then the LORD God said, 'See, the man has become like one of us, knowing good and evil; and now, he might reach out his hand and take also from the tree of life and eat, and live forever.'"

Exercise 2: What do you think about the idea of becoming like God? Since we have knowledge of good and evil, are we in the position of being equal to God?

Shortly after disobeying, Adam and Eve realized they were naked and tried to cover themselves. Then the most amazing thing occurred—they heard God walking in the garden and calling to them. He asked them where they were. Surely the omnipresent God knew where they were, but He allowed them to respond, just as He does for each of us today.

"In terms of the attributes of God, one should call attention to the striking balance of transcendence and immanence in the biblical presentation. God is the One who surpasses all that we know and yet at the same time stoops to be with us."[2]

Exercise 3: Here are verses that tell us God "walked" and "spoke." How does the garden experience differ from the incarnation of Jesus who walked among us and taught? How does this story speak to your faith?

Exercise 4: Does God speak to today's believer? How have you experienced God speaking in your life?

God can appear in any form that meets our need. There are a few times when God appears to people in the Old Testament. The Garden experience is the first. The Genesis passage does not tell us what form God took. At other times God appears in the form of a burning bush that would not be consumed, as a pillar of fire, and as smoke on Mount Sinai. Many of these passages initially say, "The Angel of the Lord," and later start saying that God is the one speaking. We will study these appearances in the chapters about Moses. These appearances are called *theophanies*, and sometimes *Christophanies*, a pre-incarnate appearance of Christ.[3]

God tempts and allows us to be tempted. Consider that Adam and Eve were not left to their own devices to sin. Rather, temptation was placed in the midst of the garden in the form of the forbidden tree. In Job 1:8, God allowed Satan to tempt Job, who worshiped God and was apparently living a blameless life. In the New Testament, we learn that Jesus was "led up by the Spirit into the wilderness to be tempted by the devil" (Matthew 4:1). Don't miss what this Matthew verse says; it was the *Spirit* that led Jesus away in order that he be tempted by the devil.

Exercise 5: What do you make of this characteristic of God as Tempter? Can you discern a reason why a loving God would allow us to be tempted?

Exercise 6: What forms do your temptations take? You may not wish to share this with the group, but do not refrain from identifying your own weaknesses to yourself.

<u>God is willing to hear us</u>. Adam and Eve were given an opportunity to justify their actions. God asked them how they knew they were naked, and if they had indeed disobeyed Him. But notice that after these questions, God asked Eve directly what she had done (Genesis 3:13). God's judgment was not imposed without the chance for the humans to tell their story.

PUNISHMENTS FOR DISOBEDIENCE

<u>God passes judgment</u>. These judgment passages are written in the form of poetry, leaving us with the need to read through the verses several times to gain a full appreciation.[4] Repetition will allow English speakers to more greatly appreciate Hebrew poetry which differs in form and intent from most English poetry. "Parallelism is the chief characteristic of biblical poetry…there is a great use of certain types of rhetorical devices. These are parallelism, rhythm, a rich use of imagery, and figures of speech."[5] The punishments are presented in parallel form: first the serpent, then Eve, and finally Adam. Imagery is rich, especially in the poetry regarding the serpent; the poem provides mental images of the serpent crawling upon its belly, eating dust, and having its head struck by humans.

Exercise 7: Do you think of the poetic books—Job, Psalms, Proverbs, Ecclesiastes, and Song of Solomon—in the same way as you think of the remainder of the Bible?

The first punishment, or curse, was directed to the serpent that God made to crawl on its belly. The New Revised Standard Version (NRSV) says "serpent" and not "snake." This is an important distinction for those who appreciate the role snakes play in the ecosystem. Snakes have such a bad reputation that people kill them indiscriminately. In Matthew 10:16, Jesus tells his disciples to be as wise as serpents, rather than as wise as snakes. Surely, we do not believe today that the snake is the epitome of wisdom! Rather, the personification of evil to which Jesus referred using the metaphor of serpent, was Satan.

Perhaps the fear humans have about snakes—some of which is justified—comes from the Eden story. But it was Satan, an entity described as crafty, who conversed with the woman and tempted her. The story would not have been as impressive if the Tempter was a rabbit or a kitten! The early scribes may have depicted Satan in this way because for a primitive people without access to antivenom, the snake conveyed strong emotional content as the personification of evil.

Exercise 8: Do you think about Satan? If so, how do you envision this entity? If not, to what do you attribute the source of your temptations?

Just a reminder here for the reader: the purpose of these early creation stories is **to convey profound truths.** They are just as important whether you believe they are literally true, or whether you believe they—like parables of Jesus— were used to teach and inspire. They are designed to tell us something about ourselves, about the God of creation, and about our relationship with God.

History was perceived differently in ancient times than it is today. Up until the time of Herodotus of Halicarnassus (484-425 /BC) the causality of events was attributed to the gods of whatever civilization was being considered. Now objectivity is the goal for the recording of events in 21st century Western life. Even in today's world, the version of history embraced by any nation is determined to a great extent by which country is the more powerful, usually meaning which country has won the war.[6]

Multiple important threads can be identified within these biblical texts written many 100's of years after humans were created. These threads include the relationship between God and His people, the lives of the primary characters, the sequence of events, and other important life components. These stories were designed to convey to the reader Israel's relationship to God wrapped in concepts that were meaningful to the people for that time. With discernment, these passages can provide sacred and guiding truths for our times as well. We need not reject them because of talking serpents and forbidden fruit if we see beyond the imagery to the essential elements of the stories, just as we do not reject the parables of Jesus.

Exercise 9: Discuss your beliefs about the disobedient actions which took place in the garden. Focus on their importance for the believer.

The next part of God's judgment is directed toward the woman but is not stated as a curse. It is a statement of fact: childbirth will be difficult. This does not mean that women should avoid childbearing or refuse epidurals during labor.

The punishment for Eve also speaks of desire and makes her husband her master. The word *master* is easily interpreted to relate to a sexual context since it is so closely associated with desire and childbirth. Surely, we are not meant to believe that a woman's desire for her husband is a punishment. Perhaps it means that the woman will desire sex with her husband, but the result will be difficult childbirth.

Some interpret this passage to mean that all men are masters of all women. This interpretation is extremely self-serving on the part of any one, male or female, who embraces it. When seen in the context of all of Scripture, "submissive" verses relate to husbands and wives rather than to the larger community of humanity (Ephesians 5). But in Ephesians, prefacing the statement that wives should be subject to husbands and husbands should love their wives as Christ loved the church, we are told to be mutually submission to one another. In other words, mutual submission is the ideal (verse 21).

It is dangerous to interpret this punishment of Eve too broadly. <u>After</u> sin entered the world, there have followed centuries in which men have dominated women physically, and in which miscarriage of justice through denial of rights, of education, and of equal payment for equal work have occurred. Placing men as masters of all things over women results from a willful disobedience of God and not from the original plan when both sexes were created in God's image. For example, no scripture passage requires that women be paid less than men for doing the same work. No scripture tells us that women should be stoned to death when they are raped, a practice which occurs even in the 21st century.

Tova Bernbaurn, a Jewish feminist, speaks of the Genesis 3 passage as,

> The offensive notion that a woman can provoke rape or molestation by the way she looks is also a byproduct of this mentality. This thought pattern exists in non-biblical societies as well. The laws in many Muslim countries that require women to cover up from head to toe are clearly based on a fear of women's influence.[7]

Making rape the woman's fault seems to give women great sexual power over men, a clear deviation from Genesis 3:16 in scripture.

For Adam, God's statements are of the "curse" variety, but the curse is for the ground, not for the man. The very ground from whence he came will be his punishment for he must toil to produce food and overcome the thorns and thistles. We are not to conclude that work itself is a curse; God worked for six days during creation and gave each of the two humans a mission for their work. Adam's original mission involved work to tend and keep the garden of Eden; outside the garden that work would be harder. John 5:17 tells us that work was done by both God the Father and Jesus the Son.

Exercise 10: Discuss the connection that God allowed to remain between Adam and the ground.

It seems that the outcome of disobedience here for both primitive humans revolves around their roles in life. She will be the mother, he will be the provider, and neither role will be easy.

Exercise 11: Discuss the two curses and the one punishment in this chapter. What do they tell us about God? Are they reasonable and fair?

RESOLUTION

God forgives and restores. In other Old Testament passages involving God's covenant people—the Israelites, there is a cycle of disobedience, forgiveness, and covenant renewal. But the Eden story happens prior to the establishment of God's covenant with his people. Does this mean that God never forgave the original Eden occupants? No. Rather the resolution of the fall of humankind through disobedience is recorded in Revelation 22:2 where the writer describes a vision of the perfected existence of God's people, the forgiveness, and restoration. In the Revelation passage, there are two trees of life, the purpose of which is the healing of nations. Hence, the Word of God moves from the first humans' disobedience to the redemption of the nations of the earth.

Exercise 12: If Adam and Eve represent the beginning of humankind—the beginning of nations—to what does the Revelation reappearance of the two trees of life speak?

THE FIRST MURDER

Exercise 13: Have someone in the group read the fourth chapter of Genesis.

God imposes justice—the first murder. The story of the brothers Cain and Abel is the first of several "brother stories" in Genesis. There are stories of the twins Jacob and Esau, and of Joseph with his many brothers. All three stories involve betrayal.

Exercise 14: What is it about siblings that results in such intense behaviors?

Was the motive for Abel's murder solely because of the response of God to the offerings, or was there something else going on? In other words, why commit murder? Why not just move on or do something less drastic? The reader of Genesis is not provided with a script of the conversation that took place between the brothers, just that God respected one gift and not the other. There probably was significantly more said than we know.

Cain is a farmer whose life involves ownership of cropland and, possibly, accumulated wealth. Abel appears to be a nomadic herdsman who moves with his animals to wherever their food can be found. The brothers sacrifice to God, each out of his possibilities. McLaren postulates that Abel's flocks may have wandered onto Cain's croplands. Cain may have seen Abel as a trespasser. Rivalry, resentment, and murder are introduced into scripture.[8] We cannot know exactly what the provocations were, but something caused extreme anger leading to murder.

Genesis 4:4-5 speaks of regard that God had for Abel but not for Cain—God was pleased with one but not the other. This first brother story provides the reader with several perplexing questions since up to this point in the Genesis narrative, God has not required sacrificial gifts. Why did Cain and Abel offer their sacrifices? Also, there is not yet a commandment against murder. Perhaps when the humans ate from the tree of the knowledge of good and evil, consciousness of moral behavior was given. Why does God respect a blood sacrifice more than a crop sacrifice?

Exercise 15: Discuss what it would mean to you personally for God to be pleased with you, or for you to have God's regard.

Exercise 16: Are we supposed to offer some form of sacrifice to God today? Have you had to sacrifice anything because of your faith?

God judges. In the King James Version (KJV) of Genesis 4:7 God says to Cain, "And unto thee shall be his desire, and thou shalt rule over him." These are the same words God spoke to Eve when casting her from Eden (Genesis 3:16). The KJV Eve verse has been long interpreted to mean that men are to be masters over women. However, in this fourth chapter, the words are spoken about two brothers, the elder and the younger. The NRSV statement for Cain is somewhat different: "Sin is lurking at the door; its desire is for you, but you must master it." This is a dire warning for all people—sin can master our lives if we are not vigilant.

It may be that we misinterpret the meaning of both the Eve and Cain passages. These two statements about masters may beg some reevaluation of the relationship between men and women, between older and younger siblings, and ultimately between each of us and our sinful natures.

Exercise 17: Discuss the Christian's approach to power over others.

God is merciful. Here again, as with Adam and Eve, God questioned Cain and gave him a chance to respond. God did not impose the death penalty on Cain for this murder. The first part of the punishment was that Cain would have trouble working the ground, similar to his father's punishment. Cain was then banished just as Adam had been sent from Eden. Cain complained that the punishment was too much to bear and he would have to hide himself from God's presence. Furthermore, Cain feared that anyone who met him would want to kill him. But note this: Mercy is shown by God to this murderer. When Cain expressed his fear, God gave him a mark to prevent anyone from killing him. Cain was granted mercy and grace, but still had to bear the consequences of his actions.

Exercise 18: Discuss the meaning of this sentence: The wrath of God is lived out in the consequences of our choices.

God examines motivations as well as deeds. The most ancient written account of the murder of Abel by Cain is found in the Dead Sea Scrolls, first century BCE.[9] The murderous act is also spoken of in the New Testament (I John 3:12 and Jude 1:11) where Abel is used as an example of righteousness. The I John reference notes that even the emotion of hating one's brother is equivalent to murder. In Jude, Cain is listed among others as examples of wrong behavior.

Exercise 19: Consider what it means to forgive someone who has wronged you. Does forgiveness mean that all consequences are wiped away?

Christian art for centuries showed the evil brother, Cain, as a bearded Jew but the good brother, Abel, as a blonde Gentile. This dissonance resulted from the blame Christians placed on Jews for the crucifixion of Jesus and was used as an excuse to persecute Jews.[6,9] It is time for people of faith to discard such prejudices and realize the worth of all peoples.

Exercise 20: Discuss how you deal with racial, gender, or religious bias in your life. This discussion can take the form of how you yourself feel, or it can focus on biases others may have.

CONCLUSION

We have learned in this chapter that God's judgment is tempered with mercy. There has not been an absolute punishment—death—imposed for every wrong committed. For this mercy we must be supremely grateful since we continue in our own defiance. More examples of God's judgment are found in the first two books of the Bible, and will be explored in the following lessons.

REFERENCES

1. Pinnock, C.H., & Brown, D. (1998). *Theological crossfire: An evangelical/liberal dialogue*, p 63.
2. Pinnock & Brown, p 65.
3. _____. (n.d.). What is a theophany? What is a Christophany? Got Questions. Retrieved from https://www.gotquestions.org/theophany-Christophany.html .
4. Salmon, P. (n.d.). How to Analyze a Poem. *The Learning Center* Retrieved from https://www.vaniercollege.qc.ca/tlc/tipsheets/reading-and-analyzing/how-to-analyze-a-poem.pdf.
5. Baxter, J.S. (1960). *Explore the book*, Zondervan, Grand Rapids, pp. 110-111.

6. Mark, J.J. (2009). *Herodotus: Definition.* Retrieved from https://www.ancient.eu/herodotus/.
7. Bernbaum, T. (n.d.). The curse of Eve: A Jewish perspective on women in society. *The Jewish Woman Organization.* Retrieved from http://www.chabad.org/theJewishWoman/article_cdo/aid/90765/jewish/The-Curse-of-Eve.htm.
8. McLaren, B. (2010). *We make the road by walking.* New York: Hachette publishers.
9. Kugel, J. (1998). *Traditions of the Bible: A guide to the Bible as it was at the start of the common era.* Cambridge, MA: Harvard University Press.

CHAPTER 2

LEADER'S GUIDE: JUDGMENT— BANISHMENT AND MURDER
GENESIS 3–4

PRELIMINARY THOUGHTS

This lesson was designed to take at least two hours and can be used for two or more consecutive meetings.

THE FIRST DISOBEDIENCE

Exercise 1: Have someone in the group read Genesis 3:6–24.

Exercise 2: What do you think about the idea of becoming like God? Since we have knowledge of good and evil, are we in the position of being equal to God?

It seems from this verse that humans missed eating of the fruit of the Tree of Life and thereby gaining eternal life right from the beginning of creation, but God provided for us to have eternal life another way, through Jesus. The difference is that the first option—eating of the tree's fruit—could be achieved through direct, disobedient action that humans could take for ourselves. The second option—trust in Jesus—is provided by God out of an infinite love for us. The rivalry spoken of in Genesis would seem to be an arrogant decision to achieve power without any help, thereby placing us in direct confrontation with God. The other alternative is being in a trusting, loving relationship with the all-powerful King of Heaven who only wants our happiness.

Exercise 3: Here are verses that tell us God "walked" and "spoke." How does the garden experience differ from the incarnation of Jesus who walked among us and taught? How does this story speak to your faith?

These appearances are not incarnations since God is not born into human form and does not continue to stay with us in the same form. Rather these are called *theophanies*, and sometimes *Christophanies*, a pre-incarnate appearance of Christ.[1]

Exercise 4: Does God speak to today's believer? How have you experienced God "speaking" in your life?

Encourage the group to share any experiences where it was believed God was encouraging them or someone they know to some action. Sometimes people will wait for others to begin the discussion; you might start by sharing your own experience of God speaking in your life.

Ask them if they think God may talk with us today? Perhaps He appears in the form of another human who just happens to be in the right place at the right time to save us from some dire fate. Or maybe He provides a word of comfort or advice which alters the course of our lives? Remind the participants that since God sent the Holy Spirit at Pentecost as a comforter, it may be that theophanies are no longer necessary for God to be present with us.

Exercise 5: What do you make of this characteristic of God as Tempter? Can you discern a reason why a loving God would allow us to be tempted?

There are several Greek words used for "tempting" including *peira* which is translated to mean "to know by experience." Another Greek word, *dokime*, is also used and means "to test the genuineness of something." *Dokime* is the word used in 1 Peter 1:7 where we learn that our faith is tested as when gold is passed through the assayer's fire.

Biblical scholars posit that the book of Job is a play written with dialogue. As such we can see the God character as the teacher of Job rather than the deliberate temper. In the end, God tells Job just who He is by asking some very provocative questions. See Job 38:4.

Paul Stewart, the senior pastor of The Gateway Church in Des Moines, tells us that the Book of Job's message is not about God but about "the unfathomably complex, war-torn creation."[2] It is about the free will that humans have and what we choose to do with it.

> If I genuinely have free will, then I can choose to align myself with God's will or go against it. God has the power to stop me—but if He always prevented free wills from doing the evil they are capable of, then He has not really given us free will and therefore genuine love is impossible.[2]

Exercise 6: What forms do your temptations take? You may not wish to share this with the group, but do not refrain from identifying your own weaknesses to yourself.

Do not force this discussion and do not condemn or offer to help someone overcome their temptations! Reinforce that we are fellow travelers on a spiritual journey and none of us have reached perfection yet!

PUNISHMENTS FOR DISOBEDIENCE

Exercise 7: Do you think of the poetic books—Job, Psalms, Proverbs, Ecclesiastes, and Song of Solomon—in the same way as you do the remainder of the Bible?

Start this discussion with Psalms because this book is more commonly thought of as songs that David wrote and sang. Were the Psalms meant to be literally understood? Compare the words of Psalms 71:13 with the words of Jesus.

Exercise 8: Do you think about Satan? If so, how do you envision this evil entity? If not, to what do you attribute the source of your temptations?

The names we use for the evil entity include Satan, devil, the adversary, *Ha-Satan* (the accuser), and *diabolos*. The *Ha* is a title as in "the satan." Have the group respond to: The purpose of these early creation stories is **to convey profound truths** just as the parables of Jesus were used to teach and inspire. Ask them where their ideas of Satan originated.

Exercise 9: Discuss your beliefs about the disobedient actions which took place in the garden. Focus on their importance for the believer.

Eve believed the Serpent. Why do we find it easier to believe the lies than the truths? Some who reject the Biblical messages, find it easy to believe in aliens or conspiracy theories.

Eve obeyed the serpent rather than the Creator. Why do we choose worldly over righteous? Do we really prefer to believe the tabloids than scripture?

Eve tempted Adam. Why do we seek to have company in our bad choices? There seems to be something pleasurable about involving others in our own beliefs. If this were not true then why do conspiracy buffs feel the need to write books, or produce TV programs?

Exercise 10: Discuss the connection that God allowed to remain between Adam and the ground.

Adam was created from the earth and given dominion over "every living thing that moves upon the earth" (Genesis 1:28). "Every living thing" seems to include microscopic living things as well. Scientists have found that some microbes in the soil can positively influence human health. "*Mycobacterium vaccae* is the substance under study and has indeed been found to mirror the effect on neurons that drugs like Prozac provide."[3] More recently, scientists in Ireland have discovered a bacterium in the soil there that can overcome the resistance developed by many "superbugs."[4]

Exercise 11: Discuss the 2 curses and the one punishment in this chapter. What do they tell us about God? Are they reasonable and fair?

Do God's punishments need to be reasonable and fair? Does the interpretation in this lesson of the curses/punishment differ from what you have always believed about these passages?

RESOLUTION

Exercise 12: If Adam and Eve represent the beginning of humankind—the beginning of nations—to what does the Revelation reappearance of the trees of life speak?

There were three trees in the garden—one tree of life, one tree of the knowledge of good and evil, and the trees from which the couple could eat. Which one did the garden "apple" come from? The two trees in Revelation are situated on either side of the river of the water of life and both are called trees of life. Is the missing tree of the knowledge of good and evil significant? Perhaps humans will no longer need knowledge of evil when we are united with God.

THE FIRST MURDER

Exercise 13: Have someone in the group read the fourth chapter of Genesis.

Exercise 14: What is it about siblings that results in such intense behaviors?

Let the group discuss their sibling rivalries as they answer this question. Some in the group may have had wonderful sibling experiences and others may be estranged. Some may not have siblings and wish they did.

Exercise 15: Discuss what it would mean to you personally for God to be pleased with you, or for you to have God's regard.

What are we hoping to hear when we enter Heaven? Is it the words from Matthew 25:23 telling us we have done well, and can now be joyful? We know from Micah 6 that what God requires of us is to act justly, to love mercy, and to walk humbly with Him. Ask the group if God will say that they have lived a humble, just, and merciful life?

Exercise 16: Are we supposed to offer some form of sacrifice to God today? Have you had to sacrifice anything because of your faith?

Discuss: "to whom much has been given, much will be required; and from the one to whom much has been entrusted even more will be demanded" (Luke 12:48).

Exercise 17: Discuss the Christian's approach to power over others.

How do you exercise power in your job? In your family? With your elderly parents? If the meek will inherit the earth, does this mean Christians should never be authoritative? Remind them that "meek" means quiet and gentle, not "weak." Meek people do not wish to fight or argue, but they can rise to the occasion just as Jesus did in the Temple. Do any of the participants desire more power in some situations?

Exercise 18: Discuss the meaning of this sentence: The wrath of God is lived out in the consequences of our choices.

Can any of them think of a choice where they decided to "eat from the wrong tree" or to "give the lesser sacrifice to God?" If so, were there any consequence of the actions?

Exercise 19: Consider what it means to forgive someone who has wronged you. Does forgiveness mean that all consequences are wiped away?

We know we are to forgive, but does forgiveness erase consequences? What if a pastor were to have an adulterous relationship with a member of the congregation and then ask the church for forgiveness (remember a TV preacher)?

Suppose you have an employee who embezzles from your company. Then you forgive the embezzler when the money is replaced. Are the consequences for the embezzler the same as your forgiveness of the actions? That is, can this individual remain in the job since you have forgiven the sin?

Exercise 20: Discuss how you deal with racial, gender, or religious bias in your life. This discussion can take the form of how you yourself feel, or it can focus on biases others may have.

If you, the group leader, feel comfortable, tackle the subject of bias against gay and lesbian people. If this could be too powerful a topic at this time for your particular group, discuss bias against another group such as women, the obese, other races, people who do not speak English well or at all...

CONCLUSION

Review the characteristics of God identified in this judgment session. Does the class agree with these? Are there additions to be listed?

REVISIT THE CENTRAL THEME AND QUESTION.

Central Theme of this lesson: God tempers judgment of humanity with mercy.

Central Question of this lesson: How does God respond to disobedient humanity?

REFERENCES

1. _____. (n.d.). What is a theophany? What is a Christophany? *Got Questions.* Retrieved from https://www.gotquestions.org/theophany-Christophany.html.
2. Stewart, P. (2013). *Thoughts on faith, culture, & missional living: The book of Job and the problem of evil.* Retrieved from http://paulstewart.typepad.com/endangeredfaith/2013/02/the-book-of-job-and-the-problem-of-evil.html.

3. Grant, B.L. (2016). Antidepressant microbes in soil: How dirt makes you happy," *Gardening Know How*. Retrieved from https://www.gardeningknowhow.com/garden-how-to/soil-fertilizers/antidepressant-microbes-soil.htm.
4. Swansea University. (2018 December 27). Bacteria found in ancient Irish soil halts growth of superbugs: New hope for tackling antibiotic resistance. *ScienceDaily*. Retrieved from https://www.sciencedaily.com/releases/2018/12/181227111427.htm.

CHAPTER 3   JUDGMENT—A FLOOD, A TOWER, TWO CITIES
GENESIS 6–19

Table 4: Characteristics of God Found in Stories of Judgment

Characteristics	Reference	Characteristics	Reference
Seeks Truth	Genesis 18:20–19:26	Despises sin	Genesis 18:20–19:26
Visits us	Genesis 11:1–9	Regrets and grieves	Genesis 6–9
Provides grace	Genesis 9:11–14	Judges	Genesis 11:1–9
Is merciful	Genesis 6-9	Expects obedience	Genesis 18:20–19:26
Is Triune	Genesis 11:5–7	Has limited patience	Genesis 6–9
Allows the world to function as created	Genesis 18:20–19:26	Can change His mind - not His character	Genesis 18:20–19:26
Cares about all creation	Genesis 9:11–14		

Central Theme of this lesson: God tempers judgment of humanity with mercy.

Central Question of this lesson: How does God respond to disobedient humanity?

THE WHOLE WORLD SINS

Exercise 1: Read Genesis chapters 6–9.

In these passages, we read of the distance humanity has moved from God. People have become so disobedient that God is inclined to destroy them all and start over. But God knows there is one righteous family undeserving of destruction and provides this family with mercy through a survival plan.

There are flood stories in most ancient Middle Eastern cultures. The Babylonian *Gilgamesh* story found on tablets in the ruins of a library at Nineveh parallels the story of Noah in many ways. It relates the occurrence of a devastating flood and a righteous man the gods told to build a big boat. He and others survived along with animals he also was told to save. The boat eventually came to rest on Mount Nisir in the same region as Noah's Mount Ararat.[1] This and other Middle Eastern stories substantiate that one or many massive floods occurred during a particular time in ancient history.

God's patience is not forever. The Lord said He would not always strive with man but then gave humans 120 years (Genesis 6:3)! This is another example of the way the merciful, eternal God views time. God is very patient even with people who embrace a wicked way of living, but that patience does not last forever.

God regrets and grieves. When God saw what evil humans were doing, He "repented" that He had created them and set his mind to destroy everything He had created. But here is a very important point—God's heart was grieved about it (Genesis 6:6). We are not told the exact reason for God's grief, but we can imagine it was because He loved us even in our wicked ways. This is an easy assumption to make because of all the evidence of just how much God loves us as shown throughout Scripture. The destruction of life on Earth was not an easy thing for God; the decision resulted in grief.

Humans undergo a very different "repentance" than that which God would have experienced in this passage. For us, the word usually means to turn from wrong to right—to turn away from evil and turn toward good. See the passages in Ezekiel 14:6, 18:30, 33:11 as well as Isaiah 45:22, and Joel 2:12–13. But for God who is totally good already, it more likely means a change of mind.

God is merciful. The flood story could have been a complete "start-over," but God saw that one righteous family existed, and did not completely give up on us. God gave Noah instructions for saving his family and the other living creatures.

Exercise 2: Focus on Genesis 9:11–14. What does God's promise about flood and fire mean to your life?

God cares about all creation. God carefully gives Noah instructions about saving the other living creatures on the planet. Noah is to take the animals two-by-two (Genesis 6:19, 7:9) or in groups of seven for the "clean" animals (Genesis 7:2) into the ark, and he is to provide food for them during the flood period. God gives Noah seven days (Genesis 7:4) in which to locate, capture, and take on board all those creatures. This may be another instance of the difference between our perception of time and that of God.

God provides grace. Readers of the Bible may come to believe that the Old Testament is all about law, judgment, and punishment of those who disobey. However, in each of the stories we study, we find that God provides grace. God has opened a way forward for those who love and follow Him. Regardless of whether one believes in a literal flood or not, the message is the same: **God loves His creation and wants the best for it. When we disobey, He gives us time to repent, grieves when we do not, and grants mercy and grace.**

THE TOWER OF POWER AND PRIDE

Exercise 3: Have someone in the group read Genesis 11:1–9.

In chapters 11 and 12 of Genesis, we are introduced to characters who existed as historical individuals. There may be components of the stories which have been added through oral tradition, but events can be supported through archeology and other historical evidence. For example, there are many ruins of large towers from the Middle East area which are called ziggurats.[2] They were constructed of adobe-type bricks (Genesis 11:3) and were found in ancient Babylon, among other places. Herodotus, a Greek historian called the "father of history," lived in the fifth century BCE, and wrote about these ziggurats. Hence, we have biblical, archeological, and independent written evidence of the existence of such towers.[3]

God passes judgment. By the time in history when people had learned to make building materials, and to construct cities, the people of Babylon were building a tower. The people hoped their tower would reach to Heaven to "make a name for themselves." They certainly achieved a name for themselves because history records them as building the "tower of Babel!"

This passage can be interpreted to be a condemnation of too much power and pride. Perhaps the Babel citizens were attempting to be like gods themselves with absolute power. This perspective is certainly valid when viewed through human history. Sir John Dalberg-Acton, an English Catholic historian, politician, and writer, put it succinctly when he said, "Power tends to corrupt, and absolute power corrupts absolutely." [4]

Exercise 4: How do you see yourself regarding personal power? Do you exercise power over others who obey you? Do you feel powerless? How important is it to you to believe you have personal power?

God visits us. Genesis 11:5 says that God "came down" to see what was going on in the city. It is recorded in a similar way as when God came to Eden. This is another example of *theophany* in which we are not told the form God took when He "came down."

Exercise 5: We think of God as being omnipresent with us. Why would God need to "come down?"

God is Triune.

In the passages about Babel, God speaks of letting "us" go down to confuse their language (Genesis 11:5-7) This and other passages speak of a plurality about God even though Jesus had not yet come to Bethlehem, nor had Pentecost occurred. Today it is reasonable for us to think of God as a complex triune being because we are on this side of biblical history. While the writer(s) of these passages did not have our historical perspective, they still had some indication that He is more than we can comprehend.

Exercise 6: Discuss your thoughts about the persons of the Trinity in light of the previous paragraph and in Old Testament passages such as the one in Isaiah 9:6.

The doctrine of the Trinity was not fully delineated until after the resurrection of Jesus and after Pentecost. Indeed, it was more than 300 years after Christ that the concept of a triune god was developed within the church. Remember that the writers of the Old Testament were not Christians; they were monotheistic Jews. But there are some Old Testament passages that hint at the triune nature of God in addition to the Isaiah passage quoted in Exercise 6 above. One of these is in the story of Abraham negotiating with God to save Sodom and Gomorrah. He is visited by three strangers who then go on to the doomed cities and seek lodging with Lot. Another inference in Isaiah 6:3a repeats Holy, holy, holy three times regarding God. The repetition of the word "Holy" appears again in Revelation 4:8. Some scholars believe that when the angels cry out the word three times, they are expressing awe for the three Persons of the Godhead, "each equal in holiness and majesty." Others note that a triune recitation is common in Judaism, although Jewish scholars dispute any idea of Trinity.[5]

God passes judgment. God did not send fire and brimstone, nor was there another flood. Rather, He created confusion by altering their speech. It is possible that God used this punishment to distribute people throughout the earth. Indeed, this was the people's fear: "We shall be scattered abroad upon the face of the earth." Having them speak a common language and amassed together in one large city did not serve God's plan for the distribution of nations.

God is merciful. Instead of destroying the people who were so arrogant as to try to reach Heaven by building their way upwards, God altered their ability to communicate. As an aside, having too many people living in one place would eventually have made feeding them difficult. The plan to scatter them allowed for both nomadic and settled farmers to have provisions for their lives. We often fail to interpret events in our lives as God's mercy, yet in hindsight it can become clear.

THE PRICE OF EVIL

Exercise 7: Have someone in the group read Genesis 18:20 through 19:26.

Genesis 13:10–12 has Lot selecting his home in the plains of the Jordan, believed to be south of the end of the Dead Sea. There were five cities in the plain—Sodom, Gomorrah, Admah, Zeboiim, and Zoar. At least one of the cities was spared due to the pleas of Lot (Gen 19:19–22). The destruction of the two cities of Sodom and Gomorrah is seen to be an entirely possible historical event although the actual geographical site is in question.

Scholars have posited the location of these cities at either the north end or south end of the Dead Sea.[6] Thus far no archeological evidence has been found of their historical existence in these areas. One reference proposed that the recorded events took place in Mesopotamia rather than in Israel based on the two cities having Mesopotamian names when translated from the Greek—Siddim and Amora.[4] However, the Mesopotamian site strains credulity when considering the arrangements between Abraham and his brother (Genesis 13:5–12). In addition, the Siddim Valley of Israel reference in Genesis 14:3 may help substantiate the southern Dead Sea location.

If they were located near the end of the Dead Sea, they would have been sitting on an impressive fault line—the Great Rift—which could have destroyed the cities with a massive quake. In addition, that area has natural gas and mineral resources—sulfur and salt. Any or all of these could have resulted in the production of brimstone, fire, and devastation. Archeological evidence for the existence of two cities, however, has not been found in the Dead Sea area as of the time of this publication. However, the veracity of the Bible is not dependent on geographical site accuracy. After all, we do not know the location of the Garden of Eden, but that does not stop us from viewing the creation as an act of God.

A word about Truth: Much has been written about "truth." The purpose of these sessions is to delve into the Judeo-Christian faith's truth about the God we worship. To that end, we accept that the writing of ancient scribes coupled with errors of translation may worry us a little about the details of some specific passages. However, the whole biblical record holds together in an impressive and authentic manner. Consider that the books of the Bible were written over centuries, but still maintain fidelity to the theme of God's greatness and love for His creation. This study will show that the characteristics of the God we worship are consistent throughout many stories, and evidenced in many lives of the righteous people in Genesis and Exodus.

God expects obedience. An interesting component of the story is the death of Lot's wife when she was turned into a pillar of salt. The Bible does not go into this in much detail, so we are left to imagine the backstory. We assume Lot's wife was too fond of the life she had to leave behind and died because of that. Bible readers may note that at no other time in biblical history is anyone turned into salt. Therefore, turning people into salt is not listed here as a characteristic of God! In addition, God's people are said to be "the salt of the earth," which is a good thing.

God seeks truth. God "heard" that great evil was happening in the two cities of Sodom and Gomorrah and said that He would go down and see what was occurring. This is the third time we have read that God was present on the earth—in Eden, in Babel, and now here. This particular appearance seems to be in the form of three strangers who first approached Abraham.

God despises all sin. We have come to think of Sodom and Gomorrah as lusty, sexually depraved places, deserving of being destroyed. The Lord said their sin was very grave. But there is only one sin listed in these passages; a gang of men wanted to rape the angelic visitors to Lot's house. Many have pointed to these verses to justify anti-gay sentiments. However, the passage is not clear about the actual sin. Is the sin of Sodom and Gomorrah about same-gender sex? Is it about rape of any person regardless of gender? Is it about hatred of God's messengers? Is it the desire to do violent harm to strangers? Since the crime of rape is more about power over another person than about sex, the real sin in this story may be hatred of those we do not understand.

Understanding of this passage is nuanced and multilayered when considered along with Ezekiel 16:49, another biblical reference to Sodom. The Ezekiel passage names sins of the people of these two cities that we as individuals might be more likely to identify in ourselves—pride in wealth and comfort, excess of food, and neglect of the poor.

Exercise 8: Where do you stand on the definition of sin? Is it breaking the ten commandments? Is stealing food to feed your starving child a sin? Is sex a sin if practiced between two unmarried people who love and are faithful to each other? Is a lie told to spare someone's feelings a sin?

There are individuals today who seem to believe that some sexual practices are more sinful than anything else we might do. This can be seen especially in relationship to gay people; homosexuals are sometimes even forbidden to become members of God's church based on this one consideration. But sex is viewed in many different ways in cultures throughout the world. For example, in some African cultures, a man and woman who plan to marry must first have sex to see if a child can be produced. If no pregnancy occurs within a specified period of time, the man is free to leave and seek another partner. This idea of "testing" for fertility is unacceptable to Western Christianity, but fully accepted by the African cultures involved. The early Puritans had a practice of "bundling" in which an unmarried couple would sleep in the same bed with a "bundle" between them. Today this is still practiced in some Amish communities.[7]

God is willing to change His mind. Genesis 18:23–32 is an amazing passage in Scripture. Abraham actually negotiated with God! But this is not the only negotiation between God and another (Job 1:1-12). Abraham asked God if He would really destroy both good people and bad people together, and then proceeded to plead with God to spare the cities if only 50 good men could be found there. When God agreed to this, Abraham went through 5 more rounds of negotiation until reaching an agreement that the cities would be spared if only 5 good men were found. Consider that it may have been far more likely to have found 50 good women in Sodom and Gomorrah!

God lets the world be.

He invites us to enter into dynamic relationship with Himself. He lets things affect and even change Him. He is not revealed as the God who cannot experience any kind of change, but as a God who wills to be our covenant partner through history with all of its surprises and fluctuations. God is involved with us in the dramas of life and salvation. Although unchanging in His character and person, God's knowledge changes concerning the things that become actual through our decisions.[8]

Exercise 9: Many believe in an unchanging God. Some biblical passages encourage us to reevaluate this perspective. What do you think?

Here are four perspectives on how God interacts with us.[9,10]

(1) Calvinism is the belief that God <u>knows and determines everything</u> that we will do and that will happen. In this belief system, God is the only cause of events and is the direct or immediate cause of everything that happens.

(2) Arminianism asserts that God <u>gives us freedom, but He already knows what we will choose to do.</u>

(3) Open Theism tells us that the future is open for God as it is for us. God loves us and desires that we freely choose to return His love; <u>He has made His plans for us conditional on our actions.</u>

(4) Process Theology holds that the future is not determined and is not known by God. <u>God changes all the time</u>. This may be difficult for many of us to accept especially since Psalms 102:12, 25–28 tells us that God is unchanging. The primary example of how God can change is that God experienced incarnation for the first time when Jesus was sent into the world. The process theology approach is grounded in philosophical reflection rather than in the Bible.

Perhaps the Sodom and Gomorrah story is simply about a loving Creator being willing to temper judgment if someone is willing to pray. We know that God wants us to pray—Jesus gave us the Lord's Prayer example in Luke's Gospel as the best form of prayer. This Genesis story provides us with the hope that God hears our concerns and is willing to weigh our desires against impersonal righteous judgment. This is a lesson for humans to follow—to consider the side of mercy over that of judgment.

God is merciful. The Sodom and Gomorrah story is another example of God's mercy in finding just one righteous person, like Noah, to save in the midst of many unrighteous people. Perhaps the lesson here is for us to be the righteous person in our community regardless of how others behave. By being that person, we may bring about redemption of our community.

Previous Genesis stories have shown us that God is merciful. It is comforting to have numerous examples of mercy from an all-powerful entity. Lot also pleaded with God for a change in plans. He told God that he could not reach the hills where he and his family were to find safety. He asked instead if God would spare one small city of the five on the plains. This was granted and Lot with his daughters reached Zoar in time to escape the fire and brimstone rained on Sodom and Gomorrah. Even Lot's wife had the chance for mercy but gave it up—if she had only looked toward the future instead of the past life. This she failed to do, showing that God's patience does have a limit.

Exercise 10: Can you think of a recent time when you were about to pass judgment on someone but changed your mind? Have you had occasion to show mercy in recent days? Can you think of something in the news in which mercy or lack of mercy was involved?

Exercise 11: When is forgiveness actually "mercy," and not just something you do to feel righteous?

CONCLUSION

The God who transcends all creation stoops to save sinners. The God who is not bound to the world nevertheless identifies with the sufferings of people. The God of holiness is also the God of love who does not keep His anger forever. God, though he is a jealous God and is intolerant of sin, yet embraces sinners.[11]

What do these judgment stories tell us about our God? He gave us the power to make choices right from the time of creation, but He is not pleased when we make wrong choices. God is patient about wrong and willful behavior, but does not always strive with us. He is willing to hear our prayers and grant our requests. God remains fair and merciful in His actions to change things; His actions are restorative and for the overall good of His creation.

REFERENCES

1. Sanders, N.K. (1964). *The Epic of Gilgamesh,* (an English translation with introduction). London: Penguin Books.
2. Davis, K.C. (1998). *Don't know much about the Bible.* New York: William Morrow and Company, Inc.
3. Crawford, H. (1993). *Sumer and the Sumerians.* New York: Cambridge University Press, ISBN 0-521-38850-3.
4. Dalberg-Acton, J.E.E. (n.d.). Retrieved from https://en.wikipedia.org/wiki/John_Dalberg-Acton,_1st_Baron_Acton
5. Fruchtenbaum, A. (n.d.). Jewishness and the Trinity. *Jews for Jesus.* Retrieved from https://jewsforjesus.org/publications/issues/issues-v01-n08/jewishness-and-the-trinity/

6. Mulder, M.J. (1992). Sodom and Gomorrah, p. 99-103. In D.N. Freedman (Ed), *The Anchor Bible Dictionary*, Vol 6. New York: Doubleday. Cited by B. G. Wood (1999) in The discovery of the sin cities of Sodom and Gomorrah. *Biblical Spade*. Retrieved from http://www.biblearchaeology.org/post/2008/04/The-Discovery-of-the-Sin-Cities-of-Sodom-and-Gomorrah.aspx.
7. Stiles, H.R. (2005). *Bundling: Its origin, progress and decline* (reprint ed.), Whitefish, Montana: Kessinger Publishing. ISBN 978-1-4179-8628-6.
8. Pinnock, C.H., & Brown, D. (1998). *Theological crossfire: An evangelica/Liberal dialogue.* Eugene, Oregon: Wipf and Stock Publishers, p. 66.
9. Humphries, F. (October, 2017). Lecture at Baptist Church of the Covenant.
10. Whitehead, A.N. (1929). Process and reality. An essay in cosmology. *Gifford Lectures Delivered in the University of Edinburgh During the Session 1927–1928.* New York: Macmillan 1929.
11. Pinnock, C.H., & Brown, D. (1998), p. 63.

CHAPTER 3

LEADER'S GUIDE: JUDGMENT—A FLOOD, A TOWER, TWO CITIES
GENESIS 6–19

PRELIMINARY THOUGHTS

This chapter is designed to last for at least two discussion periods if not more. Many in the group may never have considered an alternative interpretation of events in these passages, so you may encounter some disagreements. Work to maintain a courteous environment which allows every participant to feel safe in expressing beliefs. This study session is not about convincing anyone to change beliefs about ancient writings; it is about dialogue concerning issues confronting Christians today, and about growing in understanding of God, ourselves, and others.

THE WHOLE WORLD SINS

Exercise 1: Read Genesis chapters 6–9.

Stories of floods caused by a deity are common across many primitive cultures. Sometimes the flood is on a global scale and is intended to destroy civilization as punishment for disobedience. Flood stories are found among the Hopi Native Americans, the Incas in Peru, and in India, China, and other countries. Do the existence of other flood stories lend credence to the biblical account or deduct from it?

Exercise 2: Focus on Genesis 9:11–14. What does God's promise about flood and fire mean to your life?

Do you expect the earth to be destroyed by fire at some future time? Is there science to support this possible scenario such as global warming, a massive meteor strike, global volcanic eruptions, or will the sun become a red giant and fry the Earth?

THE TOWER OF POWER AND PRIDE

Exercise 3: Have someone in the group read Genesis 11:1–9.

Exercise 4: How do you see yourself regarding personal power? Do you exercise power over others who obey you? Do you feel powerless? How important is it to you to believe you have personal power?

The group members might speak of power currently as in their marriages or jobs. Or they may remember what it felt like to be powerless as a child. Guide them to the Beatitudes about meekness, poverty in spirit, and being blessed in the eyes of God.

Exercise 5: We think of God as being omnipresent with us. Why would God need to "come down"?

The idea of God's presence everywhere, omnipresence, is biblical (Psalms 139: 7–8) and historical from Augustine and Anselm among others. Anselm said, "the Supreme Being exists in everyplace and at all times."[1]

Where can I go from your spirit?
Or where can I flee from your presence?
If I ascend to heaven, you are there;
If I make my bed in Sheol, you are there.
          (Psalms 139: 7–8, NRSV)

But all these references—Psalms, Augustine, and Anselm—were later than the examples in Genesis and Exodus where God is said to "come down." There could be several explanations: Perhaps the ancient people perceived God's presence at different times, but did not have the philosophical idea of "omnipresence." Or maybe God related to these ancient people differently than He relates to us now that the Holy Spirit has come to us.

Exercise 6: Discuss your thoughts about the persons of the Trinity in light of the previous paragraph and in First Testament passages; examine the passage in Isaiah 9:6 that says "For to us a child is born, to us a son is given, and the government will be on his shoulders. And he will be called Wonderful Counselor, Mighty God, Everlasting Father, Prince of Peace."

The Isaiah passage speaks of a plurality about God even though Jesus had not come to Bethlehem, nor had Pentecost occurred. Christians are accustomed to hearing the beautiful version of this Isaiah passage in Handel's *Messiah*. It is an extremely inspiring musical piece and reminds us of the love and devotion we have for The Christ. However, Handel uses the King James Version which is not always entirely reliable where the Hebrew translation is concerned. A strong argument made for these words NOT pertaining to Jesus are that Jesus is the son in the trinity, rather than the Father. Jesus himself proclaimed that he was not the Father.

A different translation, reads, "For a child has been born to us, a child has been given to us; the royal dignity he wears, and this the title he bears—'A wonder of a counselor, a divine hero, a father for all time, a peaceful prince.'"[2]

Many Christian scholars have known and recognized the true meaning of this verse and translated it into English accordingly, however, their translations were not met with a whole lot of enthusiasm and thus, they did not receive the same degree of publicity as has such translations as the King James Version.[3]

This web site offers the illustration that if one of your letters addressed to a friend you call "an angel and a prince," were to fall into the hands of an historian centuries from now, you would not wish that the recipient of the letter be seen as a royal, winged personage. Rather we should be careful how we apply passages selected at random throughout the text of scripture.

All of this is not meant to say that these beautiful words cannot inspire us to think of Jesus. The case can be made for this from a devotional perspective, but not from a historical perspective.

THE PRICE OF EVIL

Exercise 7: Have someone in the group read Genesis 18:20 through 19:26.

Exercise 8: Where do you stand on the definition of sin? Is it breaking the ten commandments? Is stealing food to feed your starving child a sin? Is sex a sin if practiced between two unmarried people who love and are faithful to each other? Is a lie told to spare someone's feelings a sin?

Here are a few thoughts for the leader of this session to consider. However, there is no need to go in-depth into all of this. Have the group focus on one thing believed to be "sin." It may be anger, sex outside of marriage, thievery, or verbal abuse. But allow the group to go where it wishes for a short while.

If you need a topic to start discussion, you might ask if "marriage" is a cultural entity. Consider primitive people groups in this situation. What are the limits regarding sex that should be imposed as a membership requirement in a church? And if we set those limits, how do we get to know what is being practiced when someone asks to join a church?

Exercise 9: Many believe in an unchanging God. Some biblical passages encourage us to reevaluate this perspective. What do you think?

Read I Samuel 15:28–29. There are teachers who say that God knows from the beginning of the world what will transpire, and, therefore, the purpose of discourse with humans about something (Sodom and Gomorrah, for example) is seen as a teaching moment for humans.

You have studied the 4 ways of thinking about God's interactions with us. Share your thoughts on this matter. Finally, bring them back to the idea that God's nature, character, and desires for creation are all unchanging. But how God responds to our prayers depends on many factors.

Exercise 10: Can you think of a recent time when you were about to pass judgment on someone but changed your mind? Have you had occasion to show mercy in recent days? Can you think of something in the news in which mercy or lack of mercy was involved?

It is likely that the group will be more willing to discuss personal experiences if the group has been together for a long time. Do not force the issue. Perhaps someone has served on a jury and would like to share how they felt passing judgment about the case.

Exercise 11: When is forgiveness actually "mercy," and not just something you do to feel righteous?

If you tell others what you have done (forgiven someone), does this diminish the act as one of mercy? Do we gain something for ourselves when we forgive others?

CONCLUSION

Review the identified characteristics of God in these passages. Does the class agree with these? Are there additions to be listed?

REVISIT THE CENTRAL THEME AND QUESTION.

Central Theme of this lesson: God tempers judgment of humanity with mercy.

Central Question of this lesson: How does God respond to disobedient humanity?

REFERENCES

1. d'Aosta, A. (1998). Monologion and Proslogion, In B. Davies and G.R. Evans (Eds.), *Anselm of Canterbury: The major works*. Oxford: Oxford University Press.
2. _____, (1994). *The Holy Bible Containing the Old and New Testaments* (J.A.R. Moffatt, Trans.). Grand Rapids, Michigan: Kregel Publications.
3. _____, (n.d.). *What about "Unto us a child is born"?* Retrieved from http://www.answering-christianity.com/ac/born.html.

CHAPTER 4   THE COVENANT PEOPLE
GENESIS 12–22

Table 4: Characteristics of God Found in His Promises

Characteristic	Reference	Characteristic	Reference
Is Patient & Forgiving	Genesis 17:2–10	Gives Directives	Genesis 12:1 Genesis 13:14–17
Allows Temptation	Matthew 4:1	Cares About Names	Genesis 17:3–22
Desires Obedience	Genesis 16:8–9	Is Faithful	Genesis 15:5
Rewards Those Who Suffer	Genesis 16:10	Laughs and Desires Our Laughter	Psalm 37:13 Ecclesiastes 3:4
Has a Name	Genesis 16:13–14	Tests Our Faith	Genesis 22:1–19
Provides Guidance	Matthew 22:36–40	Does Not Trick Us	Genesis 17:16–19
Reassures His People	II Samuel 7:9–16	Informs of Future Difficulties	Genesis 15:13–16
Remembers the Marginalized	Genesis 17:21; 25:16	Provides for Our Needs	Ephesians 6:10–12 Genesis 22:14
Makes Mighty Promises	Genesis 9:11 Genesis 17	Keeps Promises	Genesis 15:5–6
Cares About the Lowliest People	Genesis 16:10 Genesis 17:21; 25:16	Prepares Us for Future Revelations	Genesis 22:6 Ephesians 6:10–12

Central Theme of this lesson: God is patient with His people and welcomes them back when they repent of their sin.

Central Question of this lesson: How does God's covenant relationship with the Jewish people apply to my life today?

PRELIMINARY THOUGHTS

God made a covenant with all creation prior to the one with Abraham—no more world-wide floods that "destroy the earth" (Genesis 9:11). This covenant has been kept; while we have had floods, there have been no world-wide floods as described in Genesis. However, this session begins with a covenant specific to the Jews. There are many references in the Bible to this covenant. Some of those references are listed here including one in the New Testament: Genesis 15:1–21, 17:1–8; Exodus 2:24, 6:4, 19:5; Leviticus 26:42; and Acts 7:5–7.

God is patient and forgiving. As we read through the Bible, we find there is a cycle involved in God's relationship with His chosen people: God chooses, the people sin, God punishes, the people repent, God forgives. This cycle happens many times.

The takeaway message seems to be that God is patient and welcomes His people back even when they reject Him time after time.

Both the Old and the New Testament speak of a "new covenant." In Jeremiah 31: 31–34 we read that the Lord will make a new covenant different from the Abrahamic covenant. Jesus spoke of this new covenant at the Last Supper when he said, "This is my blood of the covenant, which is poured out for many" (Mark 14: 24). This covenant was not just for the Jews but for all those who believe. This does not mean that God has rejected His chosen people—the Abrahamic Covenant (Romans 11:1–2)—but rather that God brought Gentiles into the new covenant. Paul told us that the Jews still hold a special place with God—they form the branch onto which Gentile believers are grafted (Romans 11).

ABRAHAM AND SARAH

Exercise 1: Read Genesis 12 and 13

God gives directives. Abraham/Abram was born in what is now Iraq. His father, Terah, packed up his family and headed for the land of Canaan (Genesis 11:31–32). They settled in Harran where Terah died before reaching Canaan. God then told Abram that he was to leave everything and travel to a place he would be shown (Genesis 12:1). This was in a time when moving was very difficult and meant herding animals through rough terrain, carrying enough food to feed family and servants, and finding sources of water along the way. Time after time Abram obeyed what God told him to do even when obedience was not easy.

After a stay in Egypt, Abram finally reached Canaan. There God gave very specific directives about what land was given to him and his family (Genesis 13:14–17) and the gift was forever. This is a source of difficulty in our world today. When the nation of modern Israel was formed from Palestine in 1948, many Arab families fled the war. When the fighting was over and they sought to return, they often found that their property had been taken over and kibbutzim constructed. Today the government of Israel bulldozes Arab homes in certain sites—such as the Old City of Jerusalem—if the families try to add rooms or do other remodeling tasks. Jewish settlements are being established on what were Palestinian lands for centuries, and this is being done against the will of the Palestinians[1].

Exercise 2: For some Christians, this governmental behavior is OK because it is seen as the fulfillment of prophecy. If this is your view, share how you came to this.

Exercise 3: Discuss how you would react should your current property be seized and returned to the native Americans who may have lived there previously.[2]

Exercise 4: Read Genesis 17.

God makes and keeps promises. Abram was told that a great nation would come from his lineage, that he would be blessed, and that his name would be made great so that all families on earth would wish to be blessed as he was blessed. This is a fantastic promise! Today, thousands of years after God's promise was made, the name of Abraham is recognized by members of the most populous world religions—Judaism, Christianity, Islam—and by many unassociated with a religion.

God's promises can be huge. God promised that Abram's descendants would number as many as the stars (Genesis 15:5). There are estimated to be 15 million Jews worldwide, making this people group "a great nation." In Israel, the only Jewish nation, there are over 6 million Jews. We can conclude from this that God keeps mighty promises.[3]

THE WOMEN

Hagar

Sarai was a Hebrew, married, wealthy, and free. But she was barren, a dishonor for women of that ancient time. She offered her servant girl, Hagar, to her husband as a vessel to bear a son. Hagar was unmarried, poor, a slave, and an Egyptian. All the power was on the side of Sarai. Hagar was bedded by Abram and became pregnant; for this ill use, she despised her mistress.[4]

God wants us to be obedient. Sarai saw that she was despised by her slave and asked Abram to intervene; he refused and put the decision back on Sarai. Then Sarai mistreated Hagar so much that the pregnant Hagar fled into the wilderness (Genesis 16:1–16). God told Hagar to return to her mistress and "submit to her."

Exercise 5: Can you apply any of Jesus' teaching to the instructions God gave Hagar to return to the mistress/master who has so mistreated her?

God rewards those who suffer ill treatment. At the time she was told to return, the Angel of the Lord also told Hagar, "I will make your descendants too many to be counted." Islamic traditions consider Ishmael to be the ancestor of the Arab people.[5]

God is named. After the birth of Ishmael, Hagar and her son were sent away permanently. When she had reached the point of despair in the wilderness, and was awaiting the impending death of her son, God spoke and promised her that her son would be the beginning of a great nation (Genesis 21:17–18). Hagar was amazed that she had survived a visit by God. She became the very first person in the Bible to call God by name—*El Roi*. It was a female, a poor person, a slave, and an Egyptian—not a wealthy Hebrew—who first called God by name (Genesis 16:13–14).

El Roi is a description of God and means "the God who sees me." Hagar's name for God is the only time *El Roi* occurs in the Bible. However, the well in Genesis 16:14 is called Beer-lahai-roi. It is much later when God tells Moses His name—*I AM*. Earlier than Hagar in the first chapter of Genesis, God is called *Elohim* which essentially means "majesty."[6] This is not His name since Elohim is also used as the name of other deities—in Sidon and in Moab. In the second chapter of Genesis, God is called *Yahweh* which is translated as "the LORD." None of these are as personal as *El Roi*.

Exercise 6: Discuss what the group thinks about the facts surrounding the first time God is named in the Bible. Include in your discussion, who it was that first announced the resurrection of Jesus. Do these facts have any influence on how you value different people?

Sarah

God cares about our names. When Abram was 99 years old, God changed his name to Abraham, and Sarai's name to Sarah. We have already encountered the importance of names with the Adam and Eve stories—they were named by God and, in turn, named the animals. Later, God told Abraham to give their son the name of Isaac (Genesis 17:3–22).

God makes promises. The story was not over after Ishmael was born because God had made a promise to Abraham and said that his wife Sarah, not just Hagar, would bear a son. God spoke first about this to Abraham rather than speaking directly to Sarah herself who was to bear the child. Abraham threw himself face-first onto the ground and laughed at God's news. Surely this was a huge belly laugh to have resulted in an elderly man throwing himself onto the ground while laughing! Was he thinking of his own sexual energies or of his wife's barrenness?[4]

Exercise 7: Do you ever think of laughter when you think of biblical stories (Genesis 17:17 and 18:12)?

God laughs and wants us to laugh. There are many verses about joy and laughter in scripture; it seems that God wants His creation to be joyful. Humans have "a time to laugh" according to Ecclesiastes 3:4. One of those times is when God does great and wonderful things for us—we are filled with laughter and shouts of joy (Psalms 126:2). But we are also told to consider our problems as joy because of our faith (James 1:2). Even Job whose life became absolutely miserable, learned that he would be able to laugh and be joyful (Job 8:21). Joy is one of the fruits of the spirit (Galatians 5:22-23), and we will be blessed with laughter even if we suffer now (Luke 6:21). Even God laughs: "The Lord laughs at the wicked, for he sees that their day is coming" (Psalm 37:13).

Exercise 8: What role, if any, does laughter play in your life? Do you experience belly laughs as did Abraham?

Abraham had his great laugh and later so did Sarah. When they were camped at the terebinths of Mamre, Abraham saw three men approach and ran to meet them, a surprising feat at age 100. He offered them hospitality and told Sarah to prepare cakes for the men to eat. One of the strangers told Abraham that Sarah would give birth to a son (Genesis 18:10). Sarah was eavesdropping at the door of the tent and heard this part of the conversation. She laughed quietly at this prediction because of her age. God heard her laughter and let her know that he knew her expression of disbelief. Later, after the child Isaac was born, Sarah remembered that God brought laughter into her life and into the lives of many who would laugh with her (Genesis 21:6).

God does not forget the marginalized. The two women in this story each give birth to a son—Sarah to Isaac and Hagar to Ishmael. A bright future for each son is promised by God. Each will be the beginning of a great nation. There are those who believe that God's blessing for Abraham was generally for all his descendants, including Ishmael, but very specific for Isaac and his generations. Ishmael, while becoming father to a great nation and father of twelve princes (Genesis 17:21; 25:16), did not receive the same blessing as did Isaac (Genesis 12:1–3), because it was through the lineage of Isaac that Jesus the Messiah would be born.

The Jewish and Christian faith histories follow the life of Isaac closely, but less so that of Ishmael. Ishmael reappears at the burial of his father Abraham, and we are told when Ishmael died (Genesis 25: 8–18). It is ironic to note that two generations after Abraham, the descendants of Ishmael, the Ishmaelites, saved Joseph the son of Jacob from dying in a pit. When Jacob's other sons left Joseph to die, the caravan of Ishmaelites bought Joseph as a slave and took him to Egypt. The story progresses to the time of famine in Canaan when Joseph saved his family from starvation. We may accurately say that Ishmael's family saved the Chosen People (Genesis 37:25–28).

Exercise 9: Read Genesis 17:18–21. In these verses, there is a promise to Abraham that his first son, Ishmael, will be fruitful, become the father of twelve princes, and become a great nation. Has this come to pass?

Islamic literature and other history provide information regarding Ishmael. Hagar and Ishmael settled in the Desert of Paran, and she found him a wife from Egypt (Genesis 21:17–21). They had twelve sons who are named in Genesis 25:12–18. His son Kedar is believed to be an ancestor of the Islamic prophet, Muhammad.[7]

Exercise 10: Do you think there is significance in the number twelve in the numbers of princes, and in the rest of scripture?

Christians should focus on the important and clear teachings in Scripture instead of seeking hidden messages or codes. We are not to seek occult meanings; "no one shall be found among you...who practices divination" (Deuteronomy 18:10–13), meaning not to try to uncover hidden knowledge by supernatural means. Those who seek conspiracy through numerology are misled.[8] The essential truth conveyed to us through Jesus Christ is that the path to salvation is not hidden from us, but rather is available to anyone who will trust Jesus as personal savior.

COVENANT PEOPLE OTHER THAN ABRAHAM AND SARAH

God informs of difficulties to come. The Hebrew people have spent time as captives, slaves, or displaced people many times in history. In Genesis 15:13–16 God tells Abraham that his descendants will be in exile in Egypt for centuries, an experience that did not start as a bad thing; Joseph and his sons went there to escape famine and stayed for centuries where they eventually became slaves.

God reassures His people. In Exodus 2:24 we learn that 400 years after they arrived in Egypt, God remembered the covenant promise to his people, and delivered them from Egyptian slavery. II Samuel 7:9–16 tells of God speaking to King David about this covenant. God promised he would give them a place of their own so they could live in peace free from enemies. The II Samuel verses were written for a people much removed from Abraham's time, around 877 BCE.

The remaining history of the Jews is one of many diasporas both large and small if one defines "diaspora" as "the movement, migration, or scattering of a people away from an established or ancestral homeland."[9] The first two diasporas were the Assyrian exile in 733 BCE, followed by the Babylonian exile in 597 BCE. The Roman exile of the Jews started in 70 CE. In 135 CE Jews were exiled, sold into slavery, and forbidden to live in Jerusalem. Jews were thrown out of England in 1290 CE, Jews were thrown out of Spain in 1492, and they were not allowed to live in Arab countries from 1948 to 1973. They have been persecuted by Muslims, Christians, and political/military leaders—this last most notably in Germany. The diasporas were later in the historical timeline, and even today when a nation called Israel exists, there is no lasting peace in the Middle East. The fulfillment of the II Samuel 7:9–16 promise has not yet come to pass.[10]

Exercise 11: The people of Israel and Judea must have thought that God forgot His covenant with them. What is the reader of the Bible to take away from this historical treatment of the Jewish people?

Exercise 12: Again, we find that God's timeline is different from what we might desire. Have you had any experience in which a prayer was answered after a lengthy time?

The Samuel books were originally one book instead of two. When translated into Greek, the book would not fit onto one scroll so the book was divided. The references from the book of II Samuel are important because they, "...have been long appreciated for their remarkable value as history and literature, and some authorities have called the author or authors of these books the first 'historian,' a title traditionally given to the Greek Herodotus."[11]

God is faithful. The promise that the Hebrews would never again be disturbed has not yet been fulfilled. There are some possible reasons why this is so. In Genesis 17:8, the promise is made to Abraham that the land of Canaan would belong to the Hebrew people forever. But there was a caveat to the promise: the people and their children for generations had to keep faith with God. Remember the cycle: God promises, His people sin, God punishes, the people repent, and God forgives. Consider the possibility that peace has not yet come because we may be in the midst of one of these cycles.

Exercise 13: In today's world there are religious and secular Jews. There are also people of Jewish descent who worship Jesus. Do you think God's promise to be the God of Abraham's people still applies? And does it apply to all Jewish people?

THE SIGN OF THE COVENANT

For reasons we may not understand, God commanded circumcision as the sign of the Covenant people (Genesis 17:9–14). Something interesting is also included in this instruction: Circumcise both "the slave born in your house and the one bought with your money from any foreigner who is not of your offspring...So shall my covenant be in your flesh as an everlasting covenant." In this passage God seems to be sanctioning slavery and coercion of slaves to be circumcised. Indeed, this passage has been used inappropriately by those who supported slavery through the ages.

Exercise 14: Does this mean that non-Jewish males serving as slaves in the households of Jews were to be forcibly converted to Judaism through circumcision?

Exercise 15: Is there a reason for Christians to obey the law of circumcision?

The early believers in Jesus had to work through the application of the Moses laws just as we must do today for some of the early laws. There are some laws in the early Old Testament books that are strange to us, some of which we in the West no longer obey. One example is making a victim of rape marry her rapist (Deuteronomy 22:28–29). Of course, the father of the raped girl could choose to forbid marriage to the jerk who violated her (Exodus 22:16–17), but it still was up to the men to decide the future of the woman! This law is still followed in some developing countries.[12] Another example of laws difficult for 21st century people to understand is found in Exodus 22:18 which says "witches" could not be permitted to live (King James translation). This verse was used as an excuse for the atrocities committed in Salem and other places by Christians. Slavery has also been justified by some of these early Bible verses, and also by New Testament verses (Ephesians 6:5; Titus 2:9).[13] Another law had people throwing shoes when they were offended (Psalm 60:8).

Exercise 16: Except for a very few biblical scholars, lay people seldom have the background in Jewish tradition to shed light on what we read in these early texts. So how are we to respond to living the Christian life when we read the laws of the Torah?

<u>**God provides guidance**</u>. Our best actions follow the example that Christ provided for us. Jesus taught us, "You shall love the Lord your God with all your heart, and with all your soul, and with all your mind," and, "You shall love your neighbor as yourself" (Matthew 22:36–40). If a person can fully obey these two commands, that person will truly be living a righteous life! A surprise to many today is that these commands are also found in the Old Testament (Deuteronomy 6:4-9; Leviticus 19:18)—Jesus was obeying the Torah laws as well as exemplifying the best of God's love.

Exercise 17: We possibly can conclude from this that God's commands to his people about slavery were to make the treatment of slaves better than they were treated by other people groups. But then why not just say, "Free all slaves now"?

Exercise 18: Have someone read Galatians 3: 26–29. Do these Galatians verses inform your discussion in exercise 17?

THE UNREASONABLE SACRIFICE

Exercise 19: Have someone read Genesis 22:1–19.

<u>**God tests our faith**</u>. There are some things about Abraham that are difficult to understand, or about which we lack information. He did not make the same attempt to negotiate with God for the life of his son that he made in trying to spare Sodom and Gomorrah. Did he tell Sarah, the mother of Isaac, what he was up to when he took Isaac on the trip to Mt Moriah? Did Abraham give even a moment's consideration to Sarah's feelings?[4] One has to wonder if Abraham said to Isaac when it was over, "You mustn't tell your mother about this!"

The Bible story is told strictly from the viewpoint that Abraham obeyed an extraordinary directive from God and never questioned. The Old Testament gives no indication of how Abraham actually felt about God's command.

God prepares us for future revelations. The sacrifice of Isaac is a familiar story to us. It speaks both of the Covenant descendants and holds a mirror to the sacrifice that God the Father made in the death of Jesus on the cross. Isaac is the only son of Abraham and Sarah, and Isaac is made to bear the wood for the sacrificial fire (Genesis 22:6) just as Jesus, the only son of God the Father, was made to bear the cross on which he would die. The discrepancy between the two stories is, of course, that Isaac was spared the actual death. However, Jesus was raised from the dead; both overcame the moment in different ways. Both are stories of incredible faith and obedience.

God allows temptations. Was God testing Abraham's faith? We have encountered situations where God allowed a test of faith for someone such as Job, and even Jesus. "Jesus was then led up by the Spirit into the wilderness to be tempted by the devil" (Matthew 4:1). This part of the character of God is hard for humans to understand. We are told that temptations help to build our own character. People of faith who pray, "Lead us not into temptation," seem to acknowledge that it is God who has the power to test us. But we also believe that God will strengthen us when we do encounter temptations (Luke 11). Perhaps God designs temptations knowing that we will be able to endure only if we rely on Him.

Exercise 20: Do you believe that it is from God that temptation comes, or is there another explanation for these passages?

Exercise 21: How does God outfit us for responding to temptation? See Ephesians 6:10–12.

God provides. Abraham obeyed the directive that God gave him. He took the son of his old age, the one promised to be the start of an entire new people group, to a distant place in order to kill him. Imagine the agony Abraham felt as they journeyed to Mt. Moriah! But the next God-intervention was to provide an appropriate sacrifice so that the child was spared—a ram was found with its horns caught in shrubs. Abraham was rewarded for his obedience to this extremely difficult request from God with a promise that the whole earth would be blessed because of Abraham's obedience (Genesis 22:18).

CONCLUSION

The God we worship is a Covenant God. It is not just the Hebrews who ask for God's help and then lapse into sin; God is at work in all creation to restore and redeem. God's great love for us is shown through the cycle of our sin followed by His forgiveness. God is constantly drawing us back to be His Covenant people according to His original design.

1. Hass, A. (2017, January 7). First week of 2017: Israel demolishes homes of 151 Palestinians, almost four times last year's average. *Haaretzm.* Retrieved from https://www.haaretz.com/israel-news/.premium-israel-demolishes-homes-of-151-palestinians-in-a-week-1.5482459.
2. *Indian Treaties and the Removal Act of 1830*. Office of the Historian. Retrieved from https://history.state.gov/milestones/1830-1860/indian-treaties.
3. Kempinski, Y. (2016, December 17). How many Jews are there in the world? *Arutz Sheva.* Retrieved from http://www.israelnationalnews.com/News/News.aspx/221859.
4. Shelton, S. (2017, June). From a sermon preached at Baptist Church of the Covenant. Birmingham, Alabama, Retrieved from https://www.bcoc.net/sermons-1/.
5. Greenspahn, F.E. (2005). Ishmael. In L. Jones (Ed.). *Encyclopedia of Religion.* Retrieved from Encyclopedia of Religion.
6. Editors. (n.d.). Elohim Hebrew God. *Encyclopaedia Britannica.* Retrieved from https://www.britannica.com/topic/Elohim
7. Schaff, P. ed. (1880). *A dictionary of the Bible: Including biography, natural history, geography, topography, archaeology, and literature.* Philadelphia: American Sunday School Union, p. 494.
8. _____. (n.d.). What Does the Bible Say About Divination? *Got Questions.* Retrieved from https://www.gotquestions.org/Bible-divination.html.
9. Merriam-Webster, (n.d.). *Dictionary.* Retrieved from https://www.merriam-webster.com/dictionary/diaspora.
10. Stefon, M. (Ed.) (n.d.). Diaspora: Judaism. In *Encyclopedia Britannica.* Retrieved from https://www.britannica.com/topic/Diaspora-Judaism
11. David, K.C. (1998). *Don't Know Much About the Bible.* Eagle Brook: New York, p. 113-114.
12. _____. (2012 July 18). The Middle East's "Rape-Marriage" Laws. *Selfscholar.* Retrieved from https://selfscholar.wordpress.com/2012/07/18/the-middle-easts-rape-marriage-laws/.
13. Glass, M. (2002). *Answers from the Bible to questions about circumcism.* Retrieved from http://www.cirp.org/pages/cultural/glass2/

CHAPTER 4   LEADER'S GUIDE: THE COVENANT PEOPLE
GENESIS 12–22

Preliminary Thoughts

This material can be used by the leader to help guide discussion. There are some points here which may intrigue participants about the women of the Bible. There is a considerable amount of history in this guide and your participants may not be interested. The information is provided in case you wish to use it.

This session is designed to last for at least two consecutive discussion periods. Work to maintain a courteous environment which allows every participant to feel safe in expressing beliefs. The hope is that all participants will grow in understanding of the God we worship and hold dear.

What is the difference, if any, between a covenant and a promise? A promise can be an oral or written agreement about something. A covenant, however, is formal. solemn, and binding. In Christianity, we speak of covenants between God and humans. Legally, covenants can be between humans, or companies, or nations.

ABRAHAM AND SARAH

Exercise 1: Read Genesis 12 and 13.

Exercise 2: For some Christians, this governmental behavior is OK because it is seen as the fulfillment of prophecy. If this is your view, share how you came to this.

Ask if any in the class have Palestinian friends or neighbors.

Exercise 3: Discuss how you would react should your current property be seized and returned to the native Americans who may have lived there previously.[1]

Discuss the fact that property can be taken from U.S. citizens either by seizure or by purchase. In the U.S., law enforcement officers can seize private property, called civil forfeiture, if they <u>suspect</u> the owners of being involved with crime and without necessarily charging the owners with wrongdoing. The owners must then prove innocence in order to get the property back.[2] In addition, states have the authority to acquire private property for the purpose of construction of roads, or walls. This is usually done by purchase, but can be done by exercise of eminent domain in some cases.[3] Relate this back to how participants view seizure of Palestinian property by the State of Israel?

Exercise 4: Read Genesis 17.

THE WOMEN - Hagar

Exercise 5: Can you apply any of Jesus' teaching to the instructions God gave Hagar to return to the mistress/master who has so mistreated her?

These are the beatitudes: Blessed are the poor in spirit, those who mourn, the meek, those who hunger and thirst for righteousness, who are merciful, who are pure of heart, who are peacemakers, and those persecuted for the sake of Christ. There are several beatitudes that apply to Hagar which we can know from scripture—she mourned and was persecuted, but not for Jesus' sake (does this count?). But we may assume that other beatitudes also apply. Was she poor in spirit or did she have an attitude? Was she pure of heart? Do any of these beatitude categories apply to the participants in the room where you are now? For example, do any consider themselves to be pure of heart? Perhaps it would be better to ask them to identify someone in the church family who they would say is pure of heart.

Exercise 6: Discuss what the group thinks about the facts surrounding the first time God is named in the Bible. Include in your discussion, who it was that first announced the resurrection of Jesus. Do these facts have any influence on how you value different people?

The participants may argue that there are prior references in Genesis about God's name. For example, Genesis 4:26 notes that people had started to use the name, Lord. The word "Lord" is a title, not a personal name.

It was women who first found the Risen Christ just as it was a woman—Hagar—who first called God by a name rather than a title. Exactly who the women were at Christ's tomb is confusing because there were a number of "Marys." Have them examine John 19:25 in order to count the number of women at the tomb. If Jesus' mother's sister is the wife of Clopas, then there were 3 women. If not, there were four.

Mary Magdalene was probably a wealthy follower of Jesus. Her name can be found in the canonical gospels twelve times—more than most of the male followers of Jesus. However, at some time in history—probably the Middle Ages, Mary Magdalene was confused with the woman called "sinner" in Luke 7:36-50 and thought to be a prostitute by most. This was later determined to be inaccurate.[4]

During the third century CE, the Jewish people stopped saying a name for God in order to not take his name in vain. Since 70 CE when the Temple in Jerusalem was destroyed, most Jews only say Adonai which means My Lord, or HaShem which means The Name. The Greek text uses Kyrios meaning Lord, or Theos meaning God.[5] There is nothing is the first 5 books of the Bible that requires God's name to be unspoken.

THE WOMEN - Sarah

Exercise 7: Do you think of laughter when you think of biblical stories (Genesis 17:17and 18:12)?

Exercise 8: What role, if any, does laughter play in your life? Do you experience belly laughs as did Abraham?

Ask them what they find funny? Is it physical humor – falls and pies in the face? Is it clever witticisms? When was the last big belly laugh? What form of laughter is kind and which is not? What is not funny to them?

Exercise 9: Read Genesis 17:18–21. In these verses, there is a promise to Abraham that his first son, Ishmael, will be fruitful, become the father of twelve princes, and become a great nation. Has this come to pass?

There are sources which deny the connection with Muhammad, or at least, indicate it is not possible to say for sure that Muhammad descended from Ishmael.[6] Does this matter to the Christian's study of the Bible? Another way of asking that question might be: Does knowing the possibility that a son of Abraham was in the linage of Islam make a difference in how you treat Muslims?

Other nations were founded by biblical persons. For example, Lot's daughters were the mothers of two nations—Moab and Ammon (Genesis 19:37).

Exercise 10: Do you think there is significance in the number twelve in the numbers of princes, and in the rest of scripture?

While the study of symbols of any kind is interesting, no one should obsess over hidden meanings. But just for curiosity, talk about it for a brief time. Ask the class to note different times the number 12 appears in Scripture. In the Old Testament there are 12 sons of Jacob forming 12 tribes of Israel. Ishmael is to become father of 12 princes. In the New Testament, Jesus had 12 apostles, and the kingdom of God has 12 gates guarded by 12 angels. These seem to be references to good things, so the number 12 may <u>represent</u> things that are good, just as "white-as-snow" is seen as a good descriptor. But this is not meant to be some secret message about which God's people need be concerned.

COVENANT PEOPLE OTHER THAN ABRAHAM AND SARAH

Exercise 11: The people of Israel and Judea must have thought that God forgot His covenant with them. What is the reader of the Bible to take away from this set of circumstances?

Remind the class that God's time is not necessarily the same as ours. Human time—the length of days—is determined by the rotation of the planet Earth every 24 hours. But God is the creator of untold numbers of rotating heavenly bodies. They do not all rotate on a 24-hour basis.

A second influence on the Jew's diasporas could be the cycle we have discussed earlier: God promises, the people sin, God punishes, the people repent, and God forgives.

God's timeline often does not coincide at all with what we humans expect. A promise of peace could still be out there in the future that God has prepared. Because our lives are destined to be around seventy or eighty years long (Psalm 90:10), we are impatient for time to be wrapped up nicely instead of generation by generation.

Exercise 12: Again, we find that God's timeline is different from what we might desire. Have you had any experience in which a prayer was answered after a lengthy time?

Allow a little time for the class to share their stories of prayers that were answered or some that are still pending.

Exercise 13: In today's world there are religious and secular Jews. There are people of Jewish descent who worship Jesus as the Messiah. Do you think God's promise to be the God of Abraham's people still applies? And does it apply to all Jewish people?

Does God's promise of salvation apply to all Christians, both devout and secular? What is the difference between secular/religious Jews, and secular/devout Christians when it applies to belonging to God?

THE SIGN OF THE COVENANT

Exercise 14: Does this mean that non-Jewish males serving as slaves in the households of Jews were to be forcibly converted to Judaism through circumcision?

This seems harsh at first glance but discuss it through ancient eyes to see that it improved the lives of many slaves. Deuteronomy 23:15–16 says that any slave who has escaped from previous owners should not be returned to those owners. Instead the slaves should live in any Hebrew town and not be oppressed. This law is unique among ancient Near Eastern lands. Be sure to note this last statement. God's chosen people were unique in their treatment of slaves; they were moving toward a kinder approach than had ever been applied. Although not perfect, the ancient people of God were being taught to be more righteous.[7]

The Talmud is the work governing civil and ceremonial laws and in it are found laws concerning the treatment of slaves. While slavery was acceptable, there were rules preventing extreme mistreatment such as the Hebrews experienced in Egypt. For example, Hebrew slaves were freed after 6 years, and they were to be treated as family members. However, non-Hebrew slaves did not come under the same set of rules.[8]

Exercise 15: Is there a reason for Christians to obey the law of circumcision?

The YES argument: We have been grafted into the Covenant people (Romans 11:17–18). Paul calls Gentiles wild olive shoots grafted onto the olive tree. Perhaps this means circumcision as part of the original olive tree also applies to the grafted shoot.

Medical science supports circumcision in that it decreases the incidence of transmission of sexual disease and decreases cervical cancer in female partners.

The NO argument: Some think that circumcision is child abuse. After all, it is a surgical removal of part of another person's body without that person's permission. Plus, we now know that babies are able to feel severe pain. As to the prevention of disease transmission, studies have found that good hygiene on the part of the male partner prevents this transmission. In addition, there can be complications from the surgery—hemorrhage, infection, injury to the penis, adhesions, meatal stenosis, inclusion cysts, and, rarely, death.[9]

What does the New Testament say about the matter? Acts 15:1–20 tells us the story of this debate Paul had with the elders and apostles in Jerusalem. People were arguing that new believers must be circumcised. Paul said that God knows our hearts, and has sent the Holy Spirit, therefore all will be saved by grace rather than by any physical sign.

When we examine what Jesus did and taught regarding the Old Testament laws, we find that he ignored many of them when what he considered to be a higher need arose. For example, he fed the hungry even on the Sabbath.

Exercise 16: Except for a very few Biblical scholars, we seldom have the background in Jewish tradition to shed light on what we read in these early texts. So how are we to respond to living the Christian life when we read the laws of the Torah?

Ask them how they apply the Old Testament to their daily lives. Then ask them what biblical "rules" they live by on a daily basis.

Exercise 17: We possibly can conclude from this that God's commands to His people about slavery were to make the treatment of slaves better than they were treated by other people groups. But then why not just say, "Free all slaves now"?

Some may argue that a sudden cessation of slavery would too adversely affect the economy. This is part of the argument made prior to the American Civil War many centuries after the biblical account. If that is a reasonable argument, what is the correct amount of time for a people group to adjust their economy minus slavery? Humans have a difficult time changing when their income is threatened. For example, we have known since the 1950s that smoking tobacco is bad for health, but many tobacco farmers continue to focus on that crop rather than spend the decades since converting to another cash crop.[10] Left to our own devices, humans get stuck in familiar ruts.

Exercise 18: Have someone read Galatians 3:26–29. Do these Galatians verses inform your discussion in exercise 17?

THE UNREASONABLE SACRIFICE

Exercise 19: Have someone read Genesis 22:1–19.

It is likely that the group will want to talk about the sacrifice of Isaac. Let them do that for a few minutes then refocus on the temptation to protect that which is precious to us regardless of what we believe God would have us do. Note that God creates life and takes life—God is the possessor of all life and was doing nothing wrong. We can guess why God asked Abraham to sacrifice his son but we cannot know the mind of God. We can only trust that this act was necessary and important.

Exercise 20: Do you believe that it is from God that temptation comes, or is there another explanation for these passages?

Give them time to offer their thoughts. Ask the class if they have ever considered the meaning of "lead us not into temptation" while praying the Lord's prayer. Was God tempting Abraham? Was God using this to teach other tribal entities (nations) in the region that child sacrifice should not occur (Deuteronomy 12:31)?

Exercise 21: How does God outfit us for responding to temptation? See Ephesians 6:10–12.

What are the opinions about "the spiritual forces of evil in the heavenly places?" Who or what are these forces, and why are they in heavenly places? Is "heavenly places" a reference to the church?

Review the characteristics of God identified in the Covenant People session. Does the class agree with these? Are there additions to be listed?

REVISIT THE CENTRAL THEME AND QUESTION.

Central Theme of this session: God is patient with his people and welcomes them back when they repent of their sin.

Central Question of this session: How does God's covenant relationship with the Jewish people apply to my life today?

REFERENCES

1. _____. (n.d.). Indian treaties and the removal act of 1830. *Office of the Historian*. Retrieved from https://history.state.gov/milestones/1830-1860/indian-treaties.
2. US Department of Justice. (2018 July). Types of federal forfeiture. *United States Department of the Treasury. Guide to Equitable Sharing for State and Local Law Enforcement Agencies.* Retrieved from https://www.justice.gov/criminal-afmls/file/794696/download.
3. _____. (n.d.) Eminent domain. *Florida Department of Transportation.* Retrieved from http://www.fdot.gov/rightofway/EminentDomain.shtm.
4. Note: See Wikipedia at https://en.wikipedia.org/wiki/Mary_Magdalene for many references regarding Mary Magdalene.
5. Paton, L.B. (n.d.). *The origin of Yahweh worship in Israel- Part I. The date of introduction.* Hartford, Conn: Hartford Theological Seminary. Retrieved from https://archive.org/stream/jstor-3140943/3140943_djvu.txt
6. CBN, (n.d.). *Is the Arab nation descended from Ishmael?* Retrieved from http://www1.cbn.com/onlinediscipleship/is-the-arab-nation-descended-from-ishmael%3F.
7. Potok, C. (1978). *Wanderings: Chaim Potok's history of the Jews.* New York: Alfred A. Knopf, p. 1124-1125
8. Hezser, C. (2005). *Jewish slavery in antiquity.* Oxford: Oxford University Press, p. 382.
9. _____. (2018). Neonatal circumcision. *American Academy of Family Physicians*, Retrieved from https://www.aafp.org/about/policies/all/neonatal-circumcision.html.
10. Bomey, N. (2015 September 2). Thousands of farmers stopped growing tobacco after deregulation payouts. *USA TODAY.*

CHAPTER 5   PROBLEMS WITH A CURSE, A TIMELINE, AND A COAT
GENESIS 9, 17, 20, 21, 33, 34, 37, 45

Table 5: Characteristics of God Found in the Lives of Ancient People

Characteristic	Reference	Characteristic	Reference
Knows our hearts	Genesis 34	Reaches toward us	Genesis 32: 1–32
Intervenes in history	Genesis 45:5–7	Can inform our dreams	Genesis 39:1–6
May leave us to our own devices	Genesis 9:20–28	Takes care of those who trust Him	Genesis 37
Cares for us even when we sin	Genesis 17, 20, 21	Does not condone slavery	Genesis 9:20–28
Gives us care of the animals	Genesis 33:13–14	Is faithful to care for His people	Genesis 39:1–6
Teaches us how best to live	Genesis 32:1–32		

Central Theme of this Session: God performs mighty and wondrous works.

Central Question of this Session: How do the events of God's interaction with ancient humans affect my life?

PRELIMINARY THOUGHTS

We have studied the big events of Genesis, the events we learned about in Sunday School. This chapter is about the in-between stories in Genesis, and can be studied all in one study session, or divided among several sessions. Some of these stories are not about God, but about the people we meet in Genesis. Other stories do involve God's interactions with humans. But they all inform us about the God we worship.

NOAH AND THE CURSE

Exercise 1: Have someone read Genesis 9:20–28.

<u>**God sometimes leaves us to our own devices**</u>. The first story is worth examining because of a terrible influence it has had on human history leading to justification of enslavement of an entire racial population. This very strange story involved Noah, who had been the only righteous man on the face of the earth prior to the flood. It also involved the first mention of alcohol. Noah planted vineyards, produced

wine, one day drank too much, and then fell across his bed drunk and naked. Ham was the first son to enter his father's tent. Ham saw that his father was naked and went to tell the brothers, Shem and Japheth. The two brothers covered their father being careful not to see his nakedness. When Noah learned what had happened, he seemed to curse the son who saw his naked body, and greatly blessed the other two.

There is confusion about who was cursed; the biblical account is that Noah cursed Canaan rather than Ham, and condemned him to be a slave to his brothers (Genesis 9:25). Canaan was the son of Ham and was not involved in the event as recorded. In addition, a curse seems a heavy price to pay if the error was accidently seeing one's father without clothing. The controversies and questions about the curse have been explored by biblical scholars for centuries.[1] This session will focus on the slavery component.

God does not condone slavery. This particular part of scripture has been interpreted by some to explain why slavery is acceptable.[1] This idea was put forth during the Middle Ages and was embraced to justify the slave trade during the eighteenth and nineteenth centuries.[2,3]

Humans sometimes blame God for things that other humans do. It is important to note that Scripture does not say the curse came from God; God had already blessed Ham (Genesis 9:1). This curse came from Noah.

The Reverend Doctor Martin Luther King, Jr. said use of this scripture to justify slavery or segregation "…is against everything that the Christian religion stands for."[4] Dr. King reminded his church, Dexter Avenue Baptist Church in Montgomery, Alabama, that the teachings in the New Testament included Galatians 3:28: "There is no longer Jew or Greek, there is no longer slave or free, there is no longer male and female; for all of you are one in Christ Jesus." Please remember that in the biblical text of this story, there is no mention of race or skin color.

Exercise 2: Discuss the "sin" of Ham and his father's reaction to it. Whose fault was it that Noah was seen naked? What if anything does this story teach us?

TIMELINE PROBLEMS

Exercise 3: Review Genesis 17:15–19, Genesis 20:1–5, and Genesis 21:1–2.

The story of Sarah's pregnancy at age 90 appears in Genesis 17. In Genesis 20 we find that Sarah was so attractive that Abraham feared he would be killed so that another man could take Sarah to wife. But it is in Genesis 21 that Sarah gave birth to Isaac. This is strange in that it is difficult to understand how a 90-year-old pregnant woman is attractive enough to cause a king to want her for himself. It is more probable that the timeline was scrambled perhaps by the scribes who wrote or copied the papyrus text.

God's word is meaningful even if humans make typos. The Hebrew Bible was constructed from tiny scroll fragments containing as little as individual verses in some cases, and from large scrolls as in the *Book of Isaiah* which is complete in one discovery, and 75% complete in another. The discovery of the Dead Sea Scrolls in 1947 at Qumron added another 200 sources to the completeness of the Old Testament.[5] The biblical books were brought together by humans who cared deeply about what they were doing. It is very possible for inconsequential errors such as chapter order to creep into the very complex Old Testament.

Exercise 4: Do you believe that a problem with chapter order negates the validity of Scripture? Where do you stand on the matter of taking the Bible absolutely literally? If you do consider everything about the Bible to be perfect, please share how you see the timeline evolving in the Sarah story above.

One can consider the Bible as a book of sacred history, written and passed down to us today in order that we may know the God of Creation and the love He has for us. It is entirely possible to be a devout believer in God and in the inspired lessons of Scripture without treating the ancient texts of the Bible as magic books. Likewise, it is entirely possible to be a dedicated Christian who believes every word of Scripture came directly from God. Perhaps it is how we live that is the ultimate consideration.

God takes care of us even when we sin. What can we take away from this story about God? In Genesis 20, Abraham and Sarah lied and said they were brother and sister. They did this to prevent the king from killing Abraham in order to take Sarah for his wife. The king did take Sarah into his house but did not lie with her because of God's intervention.

JACOB AND THE ANGELS

Exercise 5: Have someone read Genesis 32:1–32.

God teaches us how best to live. When Jacob took his wives, the daughters of Laban, his children, and his flocks to return to the land of Canaan, he encountered angels of God (Genesis 32:1–2). Up to that time, Jacob was fearful that his brother's army would seek to kill him and his household. Recall that Jacob cheated his brother Esau out of their father's blessing. The angels inspired Jacob to send messages to the Edomite country where his brother resided. The angels' visit caused Jacob to consider reconciliation with Esau. It was at this point that Jacob prayed a beautiful prayer acknowledging God's steadfast love and faithfulness (Genesis 32:9–10).

The prayer continued reminding God of His promises and asking for protection from an imagined attack from Esau. After praying, Jacob arranged for a series of gifts to be delivered to the advancing army of Esau. Then secretly in the night, Jacob sent his wives, children, some slaves, and all his possessions across the ford of Jabbok. That same night when he was alone, Jacob wrestled with someone until daybreak. The fight resulted in Jacob suffering a dislocated hip, but he would not concede the fight. At daybreak, the stranger changed Jacob's name to Israel because Jacob had wrestled and prevailed (Genesis 32:22–32). Then God bestowed on Israel a blessing.

Exercise 6: What lesson can we learn from this story? Did Jacob really wrestle with the all-powerful God? Was this an actual physical fight or was it the struggle that many must have with God over our own selfish and deceiving natures?

Exercise 7: Discuss the choice God made for Jacob to be in the lineage of God's chosen people. Jacob was a liar and a cheat. Why him? What does this choice mean for us today?

<u>**God reaches toward us**</u>. The experience that Jacob had with the stranger has been called the "magnificent defeat of the human soul at the hands of God."[6] During this long night when God initiated the struggle, Jacob encountered his own vulnerabilities—fear, loneliness, and finally physical pain. Then as Israel, he ended the night he had started in fear with a blessing from God, a fuller focus on God, and renewed faith.

KINDNESS TO ANIMALS

<u>**God gives us care of the animals**</u>. In Genesis 33:13–14 Esau wanted his brother Jacob to hurry along to be with him. But Jacob said,

> The flocks and herds which are nursing are a care to me; and if they are overdriven for one day, all the flocks will die. Let my lord pass on ahead of his servant, and I will lead on slowly, according to the pace of the cattle that are before me, and according to the pace of the children...

Jacob was concerned about the welfare of his herds. Possibly this was a selfish concern, but it also could represent the closeness ancient people had with beasts on which they were co-dependent for survival. While we do have God's permission to eat meat as well as plants, the soul-sucking problem with meat consumption has become the greed with which companies slaughter the animals. It has become a "production method" rather than the care and tending of livestock.

Exercise 8: Do you ever give consideration to how the animals that become your meals come to the supermarket? Do you specifically seek to purchase "free range" foods? Is this an important issue for you or not? What is our responsibility to the other species "caught with ourselves in the net of life and time?"[7]

RAPE AND CIRCUMCISION

Exercise 9: Have someone read Genesis 34.

An intriguing story emerges starting at Genesis 34. Dinah, the sister of Israel's sons, was raped by the favorite son of the local prince. The rapist, Shechem, decided he loved her and wanted her for his wife. Shechem's father approached Israel and offered a large bride price for the girl. Israel declared that she could not marry an uncircumcised man, and that the women of Israel's house could not marry any of the local men if they were uncircumcised. The prince agreed that all males in his country would be circumcised and he proceeded to implement this policy. When the men were still weak from the surgical procedure, Dinah's brothers armed themselves and killed every male in the city. The city was plundered and livestock taken. In addition, the brothers took "their women."

Exercise 10: If you believe that God created male and female in His image, discuss why the Old Testament talks of women as property sometimes but, other times makes them an integral part of the story (Sarah and Isaac, Rebekah and Jacob).

God knows our hearts. The local authority had decided to perform the ritual of circumcision based on his lust rather than on truly embracing the God of the Hebrews. This same kind of flawed decision does not work when proclaiming to be Christian. An example of this might be declaring allegiance to Christ in order to win an election. The decision must be genuine in order to reap the benefits of true belonging to Jesus— peace, love, eternal security, and other spiritual gifts.

JOSEPH AND HIS COAT

Exercise 11: Have someone read Genesis 37.

We have seen that there are several brother stories in the early First Testament—Cain and Abel, Jacob and Esau, Ham and his brothers, and Joseph and his many brothers. Joseph was greatly favored by their father Israel and made the mistake of flaunting that favoritism. He reported to his father any bad things his brothers were doing, flaunted a beautiful coat their father had given him in front of his siblings, and—perhaps worst of all—Joseph had the poor judgment to tell the brothers about a dream he had that his brothers would one day bow down to him. That was the straw that broke the proverbial camel's back and the brothers decided to rid themselves of this annoying juvenile. One day when the brothers saw Joseph approaching, they plotted to kill him. Reuben urged that there be no bloodshed, but rather they should throw Joseph into a deep pit and leave him; Reuben had a plan to return later and save his brother.

After this foul deed, an Ishmaelite caravan approached on its way to Egypt. Judah suggested they sell Joseph to these traders. However, the brothers were too late to implement their second plan. While they talked, some Midianite merchants found Joseph and drew him out of the pit (v. 28). These merchants sold the boy to the Ishmaelites. This transaction meant that the descendants of Abraham's illegitimate son, Ishmael, saved the Covenant people!

God takes care of those who trust him. Joseph was taken to Egypt where he became successful. First, he impressed the man who purchased him—Potiphar, the captain of the guard. Joseph was put in charge of the household where, unfortunately, Potiphar's wife took notice of the handsome young man and attempted a seduction. When Joseph kept refusing her advances, she became angry and accused him of misconduct. This is a complicated story because we have Potiphar, who some references assert was a eunuch,[8] married to a woman who lusts after the young Joseph.

This story becomes even more complex when viewed within the history and culture of the time. The fact that Joseph, a slave, was not executed as punishment, opens several avenues of thought. (1) Perhaps Potiphar believed Joseph more than he believed the wife; (2) Perhaps Potiphar valued the services of Joseph more than he valued a wife, especially if he really was a eunuch;[9] or (3) Little importance was given to the word of a woman in ancient times.

Exercise 12: There are several instances we have studied in which the hero—the one God used for good—was an inconsiderate person. Here we have a young man, Joseph, who seemed to be so proud of his position within his father's household that he lorded it over his brothers without consideration of their feelings. How do we reconcile God's favoring Joseph over his brothers?

SAVING THE COVENANT PEOPLE

Exercise 13: Have someone read Genesis 39:1–6.

<u>God can inform us in our dreams</u>. Following the unfortunate episode with Potiphar's wife, Joseph was assigned to the king's prison. While there he won favor and was subsequently put in charge of all the other prisoners, two of whom asked Joseph to interpret their disturbing dreams. When one of the dreamers—the Pharaoh's former butler—was released back into Pharaoh's service, he learned of a dream that Pharaoh had and mentioned Joseph to him. Joseph interpreted the dream to foretell of a seven-year famine that was to come over the entire region. In addition to the interpretation, Joseph offered a solution: use the intervening years to build storehouses and save grain for the subsequent bare years. This pleased Pharaoh very well, especially since Joseph gave Pharaoh the credit for the seven-year plan! Joseph was made ruler over all Egypt second only to Pharaoh.

Exercise 14: Have you ever experienced a dream which seemed to tell you what your next course of action should be? If so, did you attribute this to God or to some delayed thoughts of your own?

Exercise 15: Have someone who has experienced success in life's work address the role God played in achieving that personal success.

<u>God is faithful to care for His people</u>. God's Covenant people, the Hebrews, required saving from disaster several times in the Old Testament. While Joseph was interpreting dreams, the famine hit Joseph's family hard back home in Canaan. Israel (Jacob) asked his sons to travel to Egypt to seek help from Pharaoh. All the brothers journeyed to Egypt except Benjamin, Joseph's younger, full brother. Joseph recognized these men when they bowed down before him thus making his earlier dreams come true. But Joseph did not let them know who he was. He accused them of being spies in

order to trick them into bringing both his father and Benjamin to Egypt. Joseph had his servants secretly put the silver the brothers paid for the grain back into the brothers' packs for the return trip home, and Simeon was kept behind in Egypt.

On their second trip to Egypt, the brothers, including Benjamin this time, were afraid they would be accused of being thieves because of the silver that had been hidden in their packs. When they were greeted with a big banquet, the brothers were astonished. Afterwards, Joseph said he would keep Benjamin in Egypt while the brothers returned with more grain to Canaan. But before leaving, Judah pleaded for his father's life; he said that Israel would die without his beloved son Benjamin, the last born of his favorite wife Rachel. At that point, Joseph could no longer keep his secret and revealed his true identity.

God intervenes in history.

God sent me before you to preserve life. For the famine has been in the land these two years; and there are five more years in which there will be neither ploughing nor harvest. God sent me before you to preserve for you a remnant on Earth, and to keep alive for you many survivors (Gen 45:5–7).

Exercise 16: Can you think of events in more modern history where it seems that God intervened?

Exercise 17: Are you troubled at the lack of obvious intervention by God when events happen in which innocent people die needlessly?

CONCLUSION

These constitute many of the "in-between" stories in the book of Genesis. In these passages, we learn many essentials for our faith: Sometimes only humans are to blame for what transpires in life as with Noah, Ham, and slavery. We learn God's word can be trusted to convey profound truth even when human writing is flawed as with the timeline confusion. God is active in history to achieve His own purposes; and God is faithful to those who put their trust in Him.

REFERENCES

1. Goldenberg, D.M. (2003). *The curse of Ham: Race and slavery in early Judaism, Christianity, and Islam.* Princeton, NJ: Princeton University Press.
2. Braude, B. (1997 January). The sons of Noah and the construction of ethnic and geographical identities in the medieval and early modern periods. *William and Mary Quarterly,* LIV, 103–142.
3. Evans, W.K. (1980 February). From the land of Canaan to the land of Guinea: The strange odyssey of the sons of Ham. *American Historical Review,* 85, 15–43.
4. King, M.L., Jr. (1992). In C. Carson, S. Burns, S. Carson, P. Holloran (Eds.) Letter to Sally Canada (19 September 1956). *The Papers of Martin Luther King, Jr.,* 2-3, 37.

5. Ernst, W. (1988). *Der Text des Alten Testaments*, Stuttgart: Deutsche Bibelgesellschaff, pp.38-39. Translated into English and published in 1995 as *The Text of the Old Testament* (2nd rev. ed.). Grand Rapids, Mich: William B. Eerdmans Publishing Co.
6. Bechner, F. (n.d.). *The magnificent defect*, day1. Retrieved from http://day1.org/6297-the_magnificent_defeat.
7. Beston, H. (1928). *The Outermost House.* New York: Doubleday.
8. Peter-Contesse, R. (). Was Potiphar a eunuch? *The Bible Translator*, 47,1. Retrieved from https://journals.sagepub.com/doi/abs/10.1177/026009359604700109?journalCode=tbtd
9. Guzik, D. (2017). *Joseph in Potiphar's house.* Retrieved from https://enduringword.com/bible-commentary/genesis-39/.

CHAPTER 5

LEADER'S GUIDE: PROBLEMS WITH A CURSE, A TIMELINE, AND A COAT

GENESIS 9, 17, 20, 21, 33, 34, 37, 45

PRELIMINARY THOUGHTS

This material can be used by the leader to help guide discussion. Do not feel pressured to use every suggestion here; they are provided for use as needed to help the group consider application of the material to modern lives. Remember that all views should be heard without judgment. This study is not about convincing anyone to change beliefs about ancient writings; it is about dialogue, exploration, and strengthening faith. The objective is to have people explore the details of their beliefs and feelings about their personal faith. The hope is that all participants will grow in understanding of God whom we worship and hold dear.

This session is designed to last for at least two discussion periods if not more. You may encounter some disagreement in this session within the group. For example, some Christians are more accepting of mistakes made by scribes, and other Christians believe in a literal interpretation of the ancient documents just as they are written. Work to maintain a courteous environment which allows every participant to feel safe in expressing beliefs.

NOAH AND THE CURSE

Exercise 1: Have someone read Genesis 9:20–28.

Exercise 2: Discuss the "sin" of Ham and his father's reaction to it. Whose fault was it that Noah was seen naked? What if anything does this story teach us?

There has been controversy among biblical scholars for more than two thousand years about the nature of Ham's actual sin.[1] For centuries biblical scholars have noted that the sin of accidently seeing one's father naked was not sufficiently serious to merit a curse. But the text itself supports that the problem was simply seeing Noah naked, and nothing more. The text tells us that Ham told his brothers that Noah was naked, and the two brothers covered their father while averting their eyes so as not to look at him. There is evidence that in ancient times, seeing another's genitals was a very serious thing.[2,3]

TIMELINE PROBLEMS

Exercise 3: Review Genesis 17:15–19, Genesis 20:1–5, and Genesis 21:1–2.

Exercise 4: Do you believe that a problem with chapter order negates the validity of Scripture? Where do you stand on the matter of taking the Bible absolutely

literally? If you do consider everything about the Bible to be perfect, please share how you see the timeline evolving in the Sarah story above.

Don't challenge anyone's belief, but let them discuss. If the discussion gets heated, you might remind them of the concept of "priesthood of the believer." This concept means that all the faithful believers have access to God, and they can learn from one another. Additionally, historically reordered chapters should not prevent belief in a literal text.

JACOB AND THE ANGELS

Exercise 5: Have someone read Genesis 32:1–32.

Exercise 6: What lesson can we learn from this story? Did Jacob really wrestle with the all-powerful God? Was this an actual physical fight or was it the struggle that many must have with God over our own selfish and deceiving natures?

Was the fight in a dream or was it with a physical entity? Which is easier to believe: that a dream could result in dislocated joints or that God became flesh in order to wrestle with a human? Notice that the night started with a fear in Jacob that his brother was coming with an army to destroy him. The night ended with Jacob having a blessing from God and being physically more vulnerable. Has anyone in the class had an experience of "wrestling" with God over some problem or behavior?

Exercise 7: Discuss the choice God made for Jacob to be in the lineage of God's chosen people. Jacob was a liar and a cheat. Why him? What does this choice mean for us today?

Read Hosea 12:4 to the class. This passage says that God knows of Jacob's deeds and will punish him accordingly. Jacob had done ruthless things in his life. He deceived his father and cheated his brother out of their father's blessing. The name Jacob means "deceiver."

None of us are perfect. We should be very thankful that God still chooses imperfect humans. What does this mean for our own forgiveness of others?

KINDNESS TO ANIMALS

Exercise 8: Do you ever give consideration to how the animals that become your meals come to the supermarket? Do you specifically seek to purchase "free range" foods? Is this an important issue for you or not? What is our responsibility to the other species "caught with ourselves in the net of life and time?"[4]

Do the class members have companion animals? If so, what do they think about animal emotions and intelligence?

RAPE AND CIRCUMCISION

Exercise 9: Have someone read Genesis 34.

Exercise 10: If you believe that God created male and female in His image, discuss why the Old Testament talks of women as property sometimes—other times they are an integral part of the story (Sarah and Isaac, Rebekah and Jacob).

Perhaps the "property" talk simply reflects the culture of the time, and the inclusion of women in Scripture pushes us to acknowledge the importance of all persons.

JOSEPH AND HIS COAT

Exercise 11: Have someone read Genesis 37.

Exercise 12: There are several instances we have studied in which the hero—the one God used for good—was an inconsiderate person. Here we have a young man, Joseph, who seemed to be so proud of his position within his father's household that he lorded it over his brothers without consideration of their feelings. How do we reconcile God's favoring Joseph over his brothers?

King David was flawed. Saint Peter was flawed. What does the group think about God's choices and how do we fit into this picture?

SAVING THE COVENANT PEOPLE

Exercise 13: Have someone read Genesis 39:1–6.

Exercise 14: Have you ever experienced a dream which seemed to tell you what your next course of action should be? If so, did you attribute this to God or to some delayed thoughts of your own?

Let them have a moment to share but don't dwell too long on this point.

Exercise 15: Have someone who has experienced success in life's work address the role God played in personal success.

Success in this case does not have to be defined as financial or position power. It can be success in happiness. Did they consider obtaining the situation initially to be "luck"? Were they well suited to the situation? Perhaps, they worked very hard, taking night classes to improve or other exercises in successful planning, and therefore, attributed it all to their own efforts.

Exercise 16: Can you think of events in more modern history where it seems that God intervened?

Talk about the defeat of Hitler in WWII. There are enough human reasons for the defeat of Hitler including bad decisions on the part of Germany, the superior tank forces of Russia, and the industrial might of the United States to manufacture weapons.

However, there are some advantages for the Allies that cannot be explained by the actions of men—the weather is one. Bad weather forced several delayed battles planned by the Germans. The Dunkirk evacuation, for example, saved more than 400,000 Allied stranded soldiers. The German Luftwaffe had planned to bomb the beaches at Dunkirk where the soldiers were. That would have killed the Allies like they were sitting ducks, but stormy weather intervened. The bombing was delayed, and the thousands of Allied soldiers were evacuated to Britain. In addition, the harsh Russian winter caught the Germans without proper cold weather clothing and they were poorly equipped.

Pearl Harbor was another twist which helped the defeat of Hitler. One might not think of a situation in which 2,403 people lost their lives as helpful. But ultimately, this became a major factor in the defeat of the Nazis. America had been hesitant to enter the European war until the disaster at Pearl Harbor forced them into a Pacific war. Japan was part of the Axis powers so the entry of the U.S. automatically meant American resources helping with the defeat of the Germans.[5]

Exercise 17: Are you troubled at the lack of obvious intervention by God when events happen in which innocent people die needlessly?

Ask them about areas of famine in the world, the use of toxic gases to win conflicts, and wars where innocents are the main casualties.

Revisit the characteristics of God to see if some should be added or deleted.

REVIEW THE CENTRAL THEME AND QUESTION

Central Theme of this session: God performs mighty and wonderous works. Sometimes humans do bad things.

Central Question of this session: How do the events of God's interaction with ancient humans affect my life?

REFERENCES

1. Goldenberg, D. (2003). *The curse of Ham: Race and slavery in early Judaism, Christianity, and Islam.* Princeton, NJ: Princeton University Press.
2. Goldenberg, D. (2005). What did Ham do to Noah? In M. Perani (Ed.). *The words of a wise man's mouth are gracious*. Walter de Gruyter: Berlin.
3. de Gruyter, W, & Levenson, J.D. (2004). Genesis: Introduction and annotations. In Berlin, Adele; Brettler, Marc Zvi. *The Jewish study Bible.* Oxford, England: Oxford University Press. p. 26.
4. Beston, H. (1928). *The Outermost House.* New York: Doubleday.
5. Jordan, A. (2014). *Why the Allies won World War II.* Retrieved from https://prezi.com/mogqkrro77rf/why-the-allies-won-world-war-ii/.

CHAPTER 6 — MOSES AND MIRACLES
EXODUS 1–7

Table 6: Characteristics of God Found in the Moses Story

Characteristic	Reference	Characteristic	Reference
Is with Us	Exodus 3:11–12	Is Mysterious	Exodus 1 and 2:1–10
Calls Us by Name	Exodus 3:4	Can Become Angry	Exodus 4:12–17
Provides identity	Exodus 3:13–15	Wants to be Known	Exodus 3:13–15
Cares About Our Needs	Exodus 3:7–10	Is Personal	Exodus 3:13–15
Is Patient	Exodus	Able to Compromise	Exodus 4:12–17
Works to Convince Us of His Plans	Exodus 2:23–3:6	Is Sovereign Over the Physical	Exodus 3 and 4:1–9
Can Work through His Creation	Exodus 2:23–3:6	May Come to Us at Any Place	Exodus 2:23–3:6

Central Theme of this session: The all-powerful God intervenes in history when it is part of His sacred design for humanity's good.

Central Question of this session: What do these particular miracles tell us about God?

PRELIMINARY THOUGHTS

This is the first of several chapters involving Moses and his life. The focus here is on the call of Moses to action to save his enslaved people.

BACKGROUND AND MIRACLES

Background: A 7-year drought in Canaan resulted in Jacob packing up his extended family and moving to Egypt. He was an invited guest due to his son Joseph being a favorite of Pharaoh's. Four hundred and thirty years later the descendants were still there, but they had become a slave race.

About Miracles: It is easy to think that miracles are a common occurrence throughout the Bible. There are scattered instances which could be classified as miraculous. However, there are only three <u>clusters</u> of miracles in scripture: those associated with the Moses epic, those involving Elijah and Elisha, and those in the New Testament. This chapter will focus on the Moses story in Exodus.

In modern times, we have a tendency to use the word "miracle" often: We call any newborn baby a miracle; we proclaim a miracle following survival of a life-threatening surgery; and we may speak of the Golden Gate Bridge as a miracle of engineering. Many define "miracle" as a highly improbable happening that cannot be explained by natural or scientific laws and is considered to be the work of a god. But for the purposes of this study, "miracle" is defined as evidence that God is present and active in His creation, sometimes causing inexplicable events, and other times using His creation itself to bring about a needed change.

Some would add that the occurrence of a miraculous event should have welcome consequences. We will not attach that to our definition although most of the time it does apply for one group of people if not for all. One example of a not-so-happy miracle is the burning bush through which God commanded Moses to return to Egypt to lead his people. The command did not make Moses happy because he did not want to assume leadership of the Hebrew people.

A FLOATING BABY BASKET

Exercise 1: Have someone in the group read Exodus chapters 1 and 2:1–10.

Moses was born to a Hebrew woman in Egypt during the time of slavery. At that time, the Egyptian pharaoh who had not known Joseph, was having concerns about the numbers of Hebrews in his country. He was worried they would rise up against his people. Exodus 1:7 says the land was filled by the numbers of Hebrews. Archeological evidence in support of the Bible story is found in images on Egyptian tombs of non-Egyptian foreign slaves making bricks. These images date from the time of the Exodus in 1446 BC.[1]

When slavery was no longer sufficient to keep the Hebrew numbers in check, Pharaoh ordered all male babies to be killed at the time of delivery either by the midwife or by being drowned in the Nile. When Moses was born, his mother concealed him as long as she could. She then, in desperation, placed him in a basket she had made watertight, and put him into the Nile River.

<u>**God is the Sovereign of history**</u>. You may think that being found in a basket by a princess in ancient times is more coincidence than miracle. But consider it this way: a baby born as a slave and condemned to be murdered, became a royal Egyptian prince at the age of three months! At the time it occurred, it was only a very fortuitous happening for the baby and for the childless princess. However, it foreshadows God's longer view of history, and the delivery of the Hebrew people from Egyptian bondage. Perhaps this is another example of how God's timing may differ from ours.

Exercise 2: Can you think of another situation when male babies feared by a powerful ruler were put to death? Read Matthew 2:16–18. For more perplexing examples of the murder of babies, read I Samuel 15: 2–3, Deuteronomy 2:34; 3:6, 20:16–18. Consider the meaning of these verses for those of us who worship a just and loving God.

God is mysterious. God intervened at the birth of Jesus to save him from Herod's murderous fit. God did not command Herod to slaughter the children, but other passages of scripture involving the slaughter of innocents seem to be commanded by God. There is much we do not understand about God. Our experience is usually to trust just as Jesus' example taught us to do—he trusted even though it took him to the cross. The New Testament is filled with revelations that teach us God is righteous, holy, merciful, and loving. With that in mind, we seem to have three choices in trying to understand how a loving, merciful god can command children to be killed as found in the Samuel and Deuteronomy references above:

(1) We can simply accept that our understanding of the Old Testament passages in exercise 2 is constrained by our limited mortal vision, and our incomplete understanding of justice.

(2) We can believe that the Israelites who carried out the slaughters used God as an excuse for what they did. Indeed, there are biblical examples where God is blamed for something that He did not require. For example, in Judges 11:29–40, Jephthah made a vow to God to sacrifice his daughter which he proceeded to do. This was a vow Jephthah decided to make himself; it was never something God required.

(3) We can accept that God's longer view of history meant these slaughters were necessary for reasons that were not explained in Scripture, and for which God is not required to provide an explanation.

Just as a reminder of what these studies are about: We are trying to discern the characteristics of God! We do this because we love and worship God, and so we want to grow closer to the One we worship. However, the mystery of "God" is too amazing for humans to wrap mortal minds around. "God is neither just outside the universe nor inside it. He is simply not limited by the universe, which does not contain him. God is not just a created thing, only much bigger."[2] As we grow in our devotion to God we come to a place where human understanding is neither possible nor necessary; we decide to simply trust as Jesus did.

THE UNCONSUMED BURNING SHRUB

Exercise 3: Have someone in the group read Exodus 2:23–25 and 3:1–6.

The Hebrew slaves were being severely mistreated and it was time for God's chosen people to be freed. The Egyptian king died who had sought to execute Moses; this left Moses free to return to Egypt in God's good time. However, Moses had established a life well outside of Egypt with a wife and son, where he was neither threatened nor called to exert himself as leader of a nation.

God may come to us at any place. At this point in the story, Moses was minding his business tending the flock when he spotted a bush that was on fire but not being consumed! Moses' curiosity was peaked so he went across "to look at this great sight." At that time, the bush spoke! First, we are told that the angel of the Lord appeared in the form of this bush. Verse 2 refers to the angel of the Lord as the speaker, but verse 6 reports that God is the one speaking. The writer of New Testament Acts 7:30 refers to this speaker as being "an angel."

There are numerous instances in Scripture when angels are used to convey God's word to humans. Some Bible scholars believe this is another instance of *Theophany*, a visible manifestation of God's presence and glory.[3] The words "angel of the Lord" appear 65 times in the Old Testament's King James Version. Some examples occur in Genesis 16:7–13, 22:9–18, Numbers 20:16, 22:22–35, and beyond the Torah in Judges, II Samuel, I Chronicles, I and II Kings, Psalms, and Zechariah.

God can work through His creation. *Fraxinella* is a plant common to northern Africa and is sometimes called the "gas plant." "The name 'burning bush' derives from the volatile oils produced by the plant, which can catch fire readily in hot weather…The volatile oils have a reputed component of isoprene. The plant can catch fire with a sudden flash that covers the plant but does not burn it up."[4] While this can provide a reasonable explanation of a burning bush, keep in mind that a **talking bush is not as easily explained away!**

There may be those who see this story as contrived. However, the details provided in scripture may give us reason to take the story seriously. A fictional story could simply have God speaking out of a cloud, or in an angel appearance as was more common in the Old Testament. The use of a natural phenomenon—the burning bush which actually exists in this part of the world—is a detail that gives more support to the veracity of the story. Perhaps God felt that the person chosen to lead His people should at least be curious enough to investigate what this startling phenomenon was about.

God works to convince us of His plans. The all-powerful God could have simply ordered Moses to obey. Instead, God used the burning bush to call Moses into conversation. And in that conversation, God revealed that Moses was to return to Egypt to free his people from slavery. The Bible tells us that Moses put up several arguments trying to resist God's command.

Exercise 4: Have there been instances in your life when you argued with the Holy Spirit concerning what you knew to be the thing you should do but did not want to do? If so, what was the final outcome of those instances?

God calls us by name. There are a few other characteristics of God revealed through the encounter between Moses and God at the burning bush which are worthy of mention. God calls us by name and speaks with humans in certain circumstances in order to fulfill His plan for us. We have encountered God speaking to us previously within the Garden of Eden, and especially with Abraham and Sarah who had several conversations with God. We as humans can understand the desire to speak with and guide our children; God's desire to provide guidance to His creation is understandable.

God called Moses by name to begin the conversation (Exodus 3:4). We have already studied that names are important to God. Our own names are important to us as well. It is particularly striking that, with so many people throughout all of history, God knows our names and is personal with each one of us.

Exercise 5: Consider what it would mean to you if no one ever used your name. Is that how slaves were/are treated? Lack of the personal can make one feel invisible.

God provides an identity (Exodus 3:13–15). In this instance, God first identifies historically by referring to the various Hebrew ancestors of Moses—Abraham, Isaac, and Jacob. Shortly thereafter, God provides the name "I AM" which is *Ehyeh Asher. Ehyeh* in Hebrew sometimes is expanded to "I AM as I AM." Since ancient Hebrew did not have the tenses modern English has, this is sometimes translated as "I will be What I will be." This translation allows for us to believe that we must not expect less of God as time passes, and that He will never change on us. Another way of thinking of this name for God is "we must accept God as He Is." A literal translation into English is inexact.[5]

God wants us to know Him. A third time God provides an identity and gives the name Jehovah or *Yehovah*. It would seem to the modern reader that there really is no need to go to such lengths to identity the speaker as God since the speaker's voice is emanating from an unconsumed, burning bush! But there is evidence throughout Scripture that God makes the extra effort for humans to know Him.

God is personal. Wayne Grudem suggests an important characteristic of God regarding identity.

> In the teaching of the Bible, God is both *infinite* and *personal*: he is infinite in that he is not subject to any of the limitations of humanity, or of creation in general. He is far greater than everything he has made, far greater than anything else that exists. But he is also personal: he interacts with us as a person, and we can relate to him as persons."[6]

God cares about our needs. God told Moses that the sufferings of the Hebrews are known to Him, and they will be rescued. God promised not only to rescue, but would bring the people to a wonderful place of milk and honey.

GOD AS MOTHER

The concern for nutrition through milk and honey could be considered as a motherly concern. The following passages indicate that God the Father is also Mother:

(1) In Hosea 11:3–4 we are told that God taught Ephraim to walk, held Ephraim in His arms, and healed. God said He was like one who held a baby to the cheek and fed it.

(2) In Hosea, God is compared to a mother bear who will fiercely defend her cubs (Hosea 13:8).

(3) In Isaiah 42:14 God is described as a woman in labor, gasping, panting, and crying out.

(4) God said He bore us and gave us birth (Deuteronomy 32:18).

(5) Other references to God's maternal aspect include Deuteronomy 32:11–12, Isaiah 49:15 and 66:13, and Psalms 131:2 and 123:2–3.

(6) In the New Testament, God is like a mother hen who gathers the chicks together for protection (Matthew 23:37 and Luke 13:34).

Exercise 6: Is it meaningful to you to think of God as both Father and Mother?

THREE MIRACLES AS SIGNS

God is with us. Even though God told the reluctant Moses that He was with him (Exodus 3: 11–12), Moses continued to try to negotiate out of the job by saying the Hebrews would not believe him if he said God sent him (Exodus 3:13–14). At that point, God provided more evidence that this was an important assignment by producing more miraculous occurrences.

Exercise 7: Have someone in the group read Exodus 4:1–9

God provides our needs. Moses asked God what to do if the Hebrew people did not believe God had sent him to lead them from slavery. God provided three miraculous signs for Moses to use and demonstrated these signs in front of the burning but unconsumed bush. The first involved changing the shepherd's staff into a snake, and back again into a staff. This is the second time a snake has been involved in the early biblical books.

Miracle Number One: The Snake Staff

Exercise 8: Have someone in the group read Exodus 7:8–13.

Both biblical testaments mention snakes or serpents. The tempter in Eden is our first introduction to this image—one of the two animals that speak in the Bible (Numbers 22:28–30). There are several references to snakes or sea-serpents in Isaiah, Amos, and Jeremiah. The New Testament teaches us to be wise as serpents, that a strong insult is to call a group a "brood of vipers," and Revelations 12 talks of a snake or dragon depending on the translation.

Snakes were important in the religious and cultural lives of ancient Middle Eastern civilizations. Archaeologists have discovered images of serpents in the pre-Israelite cities of Megiddo, Gezer, Hazor, and Shechem. Snake figures flanked the doorways of a temple in Babylon, and serpent images were found in Assyria and Sumeria.[7] In many instances, evil was attributed to the snake, but in rarer instances it became a symbol of life and healing.[7] The Hebrews even held some rituals for the snake. In II Kings 18:4 Hezekiah king of Judah "broke up the bronze serpent that Moses had made; for up to that time the Israelites had been burning sacrifices to it; they called it Nehushtan."

Exercise 9: What is the group's opinion about the snake imagery? What does it tell you about God that the snake was chosen to represent evil?

Miracle Number Two: The Diseased Hand

<u>**God is patient**</u>. God continued to provide signs of His presence and the importance of the mission for Moses. God told Moses to put his hand inside his cloak and then pull it out again. The hand had become "white as snow," an interesting turn of phrase for a desert people.

Exercise 10: Discuss the use of the image of snow. What would this image mean to someone raised in Egypt for 40 years and then living in the Sinai in Midian for 40 years when he was 80 years old (Acts 7: 23–30)?

There are several references to snow in the Bible—Proverbs 25:13, Proverbs 31:21, Isaiah 1:18, Lamentations 4:7, Daniel 7:9, Matthew 28:3, and Revelation 4:14. Also see 2 Samuel 23:20, and Jeremiah 18:14.

There is year-round snow on Mount Hermon—a mountain more than 9,000 feet high on the border between Lebanon and Syria. Even before the Bible was written, the Hebrew people knew about snow because of Mount Hermon. In today's world, there is sometimes snow in Jerusalem, elevation 2,700 plus.

The use of "snow" in literature has many positive meanings, especially the association of white with goodness. It is also used to make the landscape pure and magical, to cover everything that is dirty, and to evoke silence. But snow can also represent sadness, cold, and desolation. The use here in Exodus seems to represent color that is absolute, maybe even the absence of color.

God is sovereign over the physical. The hand was healed back to its original state, but Moses persisted in his arguments. Moses argued that he was not able to speak well—too slow and hesitant. God pointed out that He alone gave the senses including the power of speech to humans; God as sovereign over all creation would give Moses the speech he needed.

God can become angry. In Exodus 4:13–14 we learn that God became angry with Moses due to his continuing arguments. Jesus, the Second Person of the Trinity, exhibited anger in the Temple, and also used the expression "brood of vipers" which one could assume is not a term of endearment (Matthew 12:34). Jesus may have learned this expression from his cousin, John (Matthew 3:7).

Exercise 11: Perhaps we should not be surprised that anger is an emotion that God experiences since we are created in His image. What other emotions does the Bible teach us that God exhibits?

God compromises when we ask. At this point in the story, God agrees to let Aaron, the brother of Moses help Moses with his speech.

Miracle Number Three: A Promise to Do More

God promised that Nile water would be turned to blood if the Egyptians did not believe. This promise was carried out once Aaron and Moses reached Egypt. Indeed, 10 plagues followed before Pharaoh agreed to let the Hebrews be freed.

CONCLUSION

God went to great lengths in working with Moses to calm his fears and convince the imperfect Moses to take on the mission. God produced a talking bush, identified Himself, called Moses by name, and demonstrated sovereignty over nature. It seems that God wanted Moses to depend on Him to provide help in the mission set before Moses. Perhaps God wants us to depend on Him still as we navigate modern life's challenges.

REFERENCES

1. Rudd, S. (2018). *Biblical archeology, The date of the Exodus: 1446 BC.* Retrieved from http://www.bible.ca/archeology/bible-archeology-exodus-date-1440bc.htm.
2. Pinnock, C.H., & Brown, D. (1998). *Theological crossfire: An evangelical/liberal dialogue.* Eugene, OR: Wipf and Stock Publishers, p. 65.
3. Bible Gateway, (n.d.). *Dictionary of Bible Themes.* Retrieved from https://www.biblegateway.com/resources/dictionary-of-bible-themes/1454-theophany.
4. _____. (2008). *RHS a–z encyclopedia of garden plants.* United Kingdom: Dorling Kindersley Publisher. Retrieved from https://en.wikipedia.org/wiki/Dictamnus.
5. Cronin, K.J. (n.d.). *The name of God as revealed in Exodus 3:14: An explanation of its meaning.* Retrieved from https://exodus-314.com/part-ii/the-meaning-of-ehyeh-asher-ehyeh/.
6. Grudem, W.A. (2004). *Systematic theology: An introduction to biblical doctrine.* Leicester, England: Inter-Varsity Press, p.167.
7. Black, J., & Green, A. (1992). *Gods, demons and symbols of ancient Mesopotamia: An illustrated dictionary.* Austin, TX: University of Texas Press, p. 166–168.

CHAPTER 6 — LEADER'S GUIDE: MOSES AND MIRACLES
EXODUS 1–7

PRELIMINARY THOUGHTS

Those with a keen interest in miracles may want to read C.S. Lewis' book of the same title. Lewis provides a remarkable, in-depth explanation in support of the miraculous events in Scripture and in our lives.

BACKGROUND AND MIRACLES

A FLOATING BABY BASKET

Exercise 1: Have someone in the group read Exodus chapters 1 and 2:1–10.

Exercise 2: Can you think of another situation when male babies feared by a powerful ruler were put to death? Read Matthew 2:16–18. For more perplexing examples of the murder of babies, read I Samuel 15: 2–3, Deuteronomy 2:34; 3:6, 20:16–18. Consider the meaning of these verses for those of us who worship a just and loving God.

Let the group discuss the three ways of understanding these slaughters of innocents. Then share this quotation from Pinnock and Brown: "We take comfort in the fact that, even in human relationships, insight into the soul of another person depends on voluntary disclosure; and not everything is disclosed even then."[1]

THE UNCONSUMED BURNING SHRUB

Exercise 3: Have someone in the group read Exodus 2:23–25 and 3:1–6.

Exercise 4: Have there been instances in your life when you argued with the Holy Spirit concerning what you knew to be the thing you should do but did not want to do? If so, what was the final outcome of those instances?

Let them share if they wish, but do not force this issue. They may wish to share a testimony they have heard from someone else about this. Remember that Paul said he did not understand himself because he often did what he wanted to do even if the action were hateful (Romans 7: 15).

Exercise 5: Consider what it would mean to you if no one ever used your name. Is that how slaves were/are treated? Lack of the personal can make one feel invisible.

Let the group consider the two questions in exercise 5. If the conversation is not forthcoming, have them consider whether or not they sometimes call people by one identifier to save oneself from embarrassment after forgetting a name—this identifier might be "Dearie," or "Sweetheart."

In the American South, there is a long-standing cultural imperative to call women "Darling," "Honey," or some other endearment. Many women accept this as appropriate. How does the group react to this? Is there a similar approach to men's names? Does the use of endearments with friends demean or enhance who they are to us? Is there a difference between the men and the women in the group regarding how they feel about this matter?

GOD AS MOTHER

Exercise 6: Is it meaningful to you to think of God as both Father and Mother?

If you are a parent, how do you function in either or both traditional roles? Do the biblical passages resonate with your own parental roles? Ask them if the idea of God as Mother is comforting or not.

THREE MIRACLES AS SIGNS

Exercise 7: Have someone in the group read Exodus 4:1–9.

Exercise 8: Have someone in the group read Exodus 7:8–13.

Exercise 9: What is the group's opinion about the snake imagery? What does it tell you about God that the snake was chosen to represent evil?

Perhaps the use of such a deadly creature imposed the need for a loving God to deliver His people from the evil serpent. Or is this more about the ancient culture's thinking about evil? Perhaps God was relating to the people's imagery in order to help them think about evil better.

Exercise 10: Discuss the use of the image of snow. What would this image mean to someone raised in Egypt for 40 years and then living in the Sinai in Midian for 40 years when he was 80 years old (Acts 7: 23–30)?

What does the image mean to you who have seen snowy weather in person, and read about its use as imagery in literature?

Exercise 11: Perhaps we should not be surprised that anger is an emotion that God experiences since we are created in the image of God. What other emotions does the Bible teach us that God exhibits?

Jesus wept. God repented. Jesus showed compassion when he would remain healing and teaching even though exhausted.

Revisit the characteristics of God identified at the beginning of this chapter. Does the group have anything to add or take away from the list?

REVIEW THE CENTRAL THERE AND QUESTION

Central Theme of this lesson: The all-powerful God intervenes in history when it is part of his sacred design for humanity's good.

Central Question of this lesson: What do these particular miracles tell us about God?

REFERENCES

1. Pinnock, C.H., & Brown, D. (1998). *Theological crossfire: An evangelical/liberal dialogue.* Eugene, OR: Wipf and Stock Publishers, p. 62.

CHAPTER 7   PLAGUES AND DELIVERY
EXODUS 7–12

Table 7: Characteristics of God Identified During the Plague Period

Characteristic	Reference	Characteristic	Reference
Keeps promises	Exodus 7:17–25	Cares about the poor	Exodus 12:1–5
Is mysterious	Exodus 8–9:1–7	Prepares us for the future	Exodus 12:1–5
Has power over death	Exodus 8–9:1–7	Is Persistent	Exodus 8–9:1–7
Cares about all living creatures	Exodus 8–9:1–7	Is more powerful than any other "god"	Exodus 8–9:1–7
Is sovereign over all living creatures	Exodus 8–9:1–7 Deuteronomy 7:15		

Central theme of this lesson: The all-powerful God intervenes in history when it is part of His sacred design for humanity's good.

Central Question of this lesson: Were the lessons learned from events in Egypt specific only to history, or can they apply to our lives today?

PRELIMINARY THOUGHTS

We continue our study of God through the story of Moses and his obedience to God's commands. This chapter involves the plagues God sends through Moses' interactions with Pharoah. There seem to be two overarching reasons for the plagues. The first is Pharaoh's derision about God when he says, "Who is the Lord, that I should obey his voice to let Israel go?" (Exodus 5:2). God responded by saying He could have banished Pharoah from the earth but had let him live in order to let people know of the power of the God of the Hebrews (Exodus 9:15–16). The second reason is seen when Pharoah punishes the Hebrews for Moses' action by increasing their work. The Hebrews wanted Moses to leave things alone before their situation became worse (Exodus 5:20–21). God then showed His power as a lesson for all—for both Egyptians and Hebrews.

Exercise 1: Have someone in the group read Exodus 7:17–25.

MIRACLES PERFORMED FOR PHARAOH'S BENEFIT

Plague One: Blood in the Nile Water

There are many who seek to explain the plagues in Egypt as natural phenomena. Since God is sovereign over nature, there is no reason to believe God could not use natural phenomena to motivate Pharaoh to free the Hebrews. But there are some plagues which cannot be explained through nature; these events require us to think beyond the boundaries of our objective existence.

God keeps promises. God had told Moses that the Nile would turn to blood if Pharaoh did not agree to let the people be free to leave. After Pharaoh's refusal, the miracle occurred. There are those who attribute the color change to red silt which periodically washed down the Nile from Abyssinia. This explanation does not hold since the red silt is welcomed by Egyptians as it represents new, rich soil for growing crops along the river. But no one welcomed the "bloody" Nile. Neither did the good silt normally stink as did the Nile when turned to blood. Another reason for considering this to be a miracle of God is the timing; the change in the Nile occurred at the time God said that it would.

In a scriptural reference to a different body of water in Moab (2 Kings 3:22), we find "water…red as blood" indicating that the water was not blood but looked like blood. What we read in Exodus clearly says the water became blood.

Plagues Two, Three, Four, and Five: Frogs, Gnats, Flies, Disease

Exercise 2: Have someone in the group read Exodus 8 through 9:1–7.

God is sovereign over all living creatures. The next plagues involve living creatures—frogs, flies, biting insects, wild animals, and cattle. Moses and Aaron used the shepherd's staff to bring a plague of frogs on the land. The frogs were everywhere, even in the ovens! One explanation would be that a river of blood would result in frogs leaving the river. If so, the frog plague resulted directly from the first miracle—blood in the Nile. Since God is present in the "natural," natural explanations for the plagues do not negate God's power or purpose.

Some biblical archaeologists note that the *Ipuwer Papyrus* told of a cataclysmic occurrence in ancient Egypt which included some of the plague events noted in Exodus. This document title translates as *Admonitions of Ipuwer* and was apparently written 2050-1652 BCE, a time which corresponds to the Egyptian Middle Kingdom era. This timing conflicts with the timing of the exodus, but both theorized timings—of the papyrus and of the exodus, are open to scholarly debate.[1]

Today the *Ipuwer Papyrus* resides in the National Archaeological Museum in Leiden, Netherlands. The document does not appear to have been written to support the biblical account, but there are intriguing mentions of similar events that are reported in Exodus. In support of the biblical account, the papyrus reads, "Plague is throughout the land. Blood is everywhere…The river is blood…Gates, columns and walls are consumed by fire…Cattle moan…The land is not light."[1]

God is persistent. Aaron's staff caused the dust of the ground to become maggots. God had used dust previously in the creation story to form the first human; the Hebrew people would have had no problem attributing this creative use of dust to God. Note that for the first time, Pharaoh's magicians could not duplicate this plague—things were becoming more serious.

When swarms of flies and their larva—maggots, were released on the land, the Hebrews who lived in Goshen were protected from this plague. This was done to show Pharaoh that "I, the Lord, am here in the land. I will make a distinction between my people and yours." The next plague, "a terrible pestilence," was released on the service animals of Egypt—cattle, horses, asses, camels, sheep. Biting flies can be found today in the northeast African continent, and these carry livestock diseases. A plague of these bugs could certainly have had the effect of killing all of the service animals. But note this: those belonging to the Hebrew people survived (Exodus 9:6).

Exercise 3: For those of us who love animals and see them as innocent victims, this plague is difficult to understand. Of course, many of God's actions are difficult for humans to understand, nor is it necessary for us to understand all that God does. Discuss why this approach would have impressed the Egyptian people with the power of the Hebrew God.

God is sovereign. Understanding God is possible only when God allows us to know Him. In Deuteronomy 7:15 God promises the Hebrew people that if they are careful to observe the laws, God will not allow any of the "foul diseases of Egypt" on them; this promise does not apply to their enemies. However, in Deuteronomy 28:58–29 God promises the Israelites in Moab that terrible things will happen—unimaginable plagues, malignant and persistent, and sickness, persistent and severe—if they do not observe the laws. We are left with the reminder that God is sovereign and obedience is essential.

Plagues Six, Seven and Eight: Festering Boils, Flashing Hail, and Locusts

God is persistent. If providing evidence of God's power through changes in the water did not work, and bringing suffering among the non-human creatures did not work, perhaps a more personal attack would bring Pharaoh to see God's power; the next plague commanded in Exodus 9:8–12 was to bring festering boils on both humans and their beasts.

God cares about other species. God showed mercy to the beasts with the next plague. A warning was given that hail with flashing fire would be sent on the Egyptians. They were told to bring all beasts and themselves indoors if they wanted to live. Some Egyptians brought their slaves and beasts, and themselves, one assumes, into shelter. The hail that followed "beat down every growing thing and shattered every tree," but nothing occurred in the land of Goshen where the Hebrews lived. Hail is common in Egypt today and can ruin the crops. However, there is no mention in today's weather reports of "flashing fire" associated with the hail.

A problem shows up here in the sequence of events. All the Egyptians' cattle died when bitten by hordes of flies. Yet in the very next plague, festering boils appear on beasts that are left outside.

Exercise 4: Have the group discuss this apparent discrepancy in Scripture.

The next plague sent by God was a horde of locusts which devoured any plants that were not destroyed by the hail. After this Pharaoh agreed to let the men go out into the wilderness to worship their God, but refused to allow women, children, and livestock to go. Moses, who had become more confident by this time, disagreed and insisted that all be allowed to go. Pharaoh stuck with his decision to allow only the men to go; this was not what God wanted, so locusts were released on the land. A horde of locusts can devour the amount of food in one day that can be consumed by 2,500 humans.[2] This plague is one that can be explained as a natural occurrence since plagues of locusts descend on Egypt even today. What makes it a miracle is the timing in which it occurred; Moses, in obedience to God, called it forth and it happened!

God is mysterious. At the time of creation, God gave us freedom of choice even to the extent of rejecting Him. But in these Exodus passages, God "hardens" the heart of Pharaoh after each plague so that he does not relent and let the people go. According to the translation, Pharaoh's decisions are influenced in a negative way by the God who loves us!

Exercise 5: How are those of us who have put eternal trust in Jesus to process this information? We may wonder why God would turn someone against Him if indeed God did this. What do you think about this passage? Is there any emotion or feeling that you believe God caused you to have?

MIRACLES PERFORMED TO SHOW GOD'S POWER OVER THE GODS OF EGYPT

Plague Nine: Impenetrable Darkness

God is more powerful than any other "god". Three days of darkness followed when Pharaoh again refused to free the slaves. This plague of darkness may have served to show God's power over Ra, the Egyptian god of the sun. There are debates about this darkness. Some say this may have been caused by a hot wind called *Khamsin* (Arabic for 50 days) that can fill the air with sand causing relative darkness. However, there is no biblical or otherwise report of such a strong sand-filled wind associated with the darkness occurring during that time frame. Other scholars say there is no reasonable explanation for impenetrable darkness lasting for even three days. Note that the Hebrew people had light—they lived in a different place (Goshen). Again, we know that God is the ruler of all nature, so however the darkness was achieved, scripture says it was through the power of God.

Exercise 6: Have someone in the group read Exodus 12:1–5. What characteristic of God stands out to you in these verses?

Plague Ten: The Final Plague

Exercise 7: Have someone read Exodus 12:12.

Exercise 8: What does the group know about the modern-day celebration of Passover? If you have Jewish friends as many of us do, do you ever participate in the Passover rituals?

God has power over death. Try as we might, there is no reasonable scientific cause for only Egyptian firstborn children to die over the course of one night. Do not forget that even firstborn cattle died. If children of many different birth orders had died, or if firstborn children of all people living in Egypt had died, scholars may have been able to provide a non-miraculous reason through genetic studies or ancient disease histories. Even if just humans had died, there could be an explanation other than miracle. But none of these is the case. The only explanation seems to be the intervention of God.

The cattle death problem rears its head again here. Remember that in Exodus 9:6, "All the herds of Egypt died, but from the herds of the Israelites not one single beast died." But here we read that the firstborn of the beasts died at this later time. This means there had to be animals belonging to the Egyptians so that their first-borns could die. There seem to be several possibilities for this discrepancy. One possibility is that since the English version Bible from which we read is not the original language of the

Old Testament, the translators could have erred. The second possibility is that the Egyptians took cattle from the Hebrew slaves to replenish their herds. Or third, perhaps a significant passage of time elapsed between the plague that killed their animals and this additional plague.

The third explanation involves the movie, *The Ten Commandments.* This movie has left us with ideas that are not necessarily scriptural. The movie depicts the plagues happening quickly, one day after another. However, this timing is not indicated in Scripture. We know that some amount of time elapsed between the end of most plagues and God's new instructions to Moses. We are not told how much time elapsed between one plague and another, but we are told that God spoke to Moses, and afterwards Moses <u>returned</u> to Pharaoh. We do not know where Moses and Aaron were staying that required "returning." We do not know how long the journey took both to go and to come back without benefit of motorized conveyance. There could have been time for new cattle to be acquired from multiple sources on the North African continent.

Exercise 9: Have the group discuss this second discrepancy.

Exercise 10: Have someone in the group read Exodus 12:1–5. What characteristic of God stands out to you in these verses?

<u>God cares about the poor</u>. Did you notice that in the midst of detailed instructions, God made arrangements for those slave families without the ability to purchase a lamb?

Exercise 11: Why did God give such explicit instructions for how to eat the sacrificial lambs?

<u>God prepares us for the future</u>. The Hebrew people were told not to wait for bread to rise, but to eat unleavened foods. They were told to eat with their shoes on and staffs in their hands. They were told to stay indoors until the morning. All this was probably because they had to be ready to move at a moment's notice when the time came to escape from Egypt.

Exercise 12: Have someone read Exodus 12:34–36. What does it mean that the Hebrews were to ask their Egyptian neighbors for the items listed in these verses?

NOTE: Miracles performed to save the Hebrew people as they escaped are found in the next lesson.

DID THE MIRACLES REALLY HAPPEN?

There are those who would argue that these are simply stories developed over the centuries to support belief in a particular deity. For people of faith, however, there is no need for objective evidence to support Scripture. When evidence is found, however, it helps to bring faith to those who have not been nurtured in a faith tradition.

Helpful Science. Our lives have been greatly enriched by science. We live longer and healthier; we have technology in developed countries that makes daily tasks easier; and our transportation systems make travels more efficient. These are just a few ways science benefits us. Most of the time we put our trust in the men and women of science. However, science is not a god, not perfect, and scientists can be mistaken or even ruthless about defending certain positions.

Velilovshy's Book. One strong example of the collision between faith and science is the way many scientists reacted to a book originally published by McMillan in 1951. Dr. Immanuel Velilovsky's controversial book supported the *Ipuwer Papyrus* as being evidentiary for the plagues in *Exodus*. His scholarly credentials were numerous and impressive. In addition to the book in question, Velikovshy's work in the field of psychiatry was published and well received, and he edited works in collaboration with Albert Einstein in the 1930s for the journal *Scripta Universitatis atque Bibliothecae Hierosolymitarum*. These distinctions were among the reasons Velikovsky could help establish the Hebrew University in Jerusalem.

However, Velilovsky's proposal about Exodus so infuriated the scientific community that pressure, in the form of boycott threats by the *Astronomical Academia*, was brought to bear on the publishing house of McMillan which then withdrew the book from sales. Fortunately, Doubleday press obtained the rights and continued to publish.[3]

Journal Publications. Many professions rely strongly on scientific publications for the advancement of their work—one example is health care. This reliance is necessary for all that makes our lives safer, more convenient, and healthier. However, each article in each science must be read with critical thinking as well as educated appreciation for the research being done. While rare, there have been cases of fraud so well done that publication occurred only later to be retracted.[4]

A more pervasive way that science can maintain power over information is that scientific journals prefer to publish articles with positive findings. One opinion is that "if journalism as a whole is bad (and it is), science journalism is even worse. Not only is it susceptible to the same sorts of biases that afflict regular journalism, but it is uniquely vulnerable to outrageous sensationalism."[5]

Egyptian Texts. At this date we know of no historical Egyptian texts in which it is strongly asserted that plagues took place. This is not hard to understand since the Egyptians were the losers in this biblically described event. Why would any nation defeated by its own slaves write this into their history? Efforts to preserve history most likely focus on the events which build up the image of a nation rather than on those events which result in humiliating losses. "The Egyptians were not above altering historical records when the truth proved to be embarrassing or went against their political interests. It was not the praxis of the pharaohs to advertise their failures on temple walls for all to see."[6]

Science versus Art. None of these examples—Velilovsky's situation, scientific journalism bias, and historical Egyptian texts—proves or disproves the biblical account. What must be remembered, however, is that people of faith need not bow to every non-believer's ideas about biblical history. There are professional archeologists who argue on both sides regarding evidence about the miraculous nature of these occurrences. William Dever says, "Good scholars, honest scholars, will continue to differ about the interpretations of archaeological remains simply because archaeology is not a science, it is an art. And sometimes it is not even a very good art."[7]

Objectivity. These examples are not meant to cause us to withdraw from the contributions of the scientific community. Rather, they should be accepted as reason for us to view anyone's ideas, whether scientific or theological, with a modicum of skepticism before fully embracing the ideas. This skepticism certainly applies to religious persons who provide leadership. The last sentence can be substantiated by pointing to radical groups who encourage acts of violence in the name of some god, or to leaders who ask their followers to commit mass suicide.

Remember that the biblical account was never written as a book of science, but one about God interacting with His creation. For faith to exist, there must be some element of doubt involved. Otherwise whatever is being considered enters the realm of objectivity rather than faith. It is logical that some plagues resulted from natural events. However, because of the way they occurred, God's involvement can be discerned.

SUPPORT FOR THE EXODUS MATERIAL

The following material recounts some things already discussed in this lesson; some new material is included. These are offered with the hope that your faith will be strengthened, and your spiritual life deepened.

Evidence for Occupation of Goshen. The book of Exodus has the Hebrews living in the Land of Goshen at the time of Moses. This is consistent with the Genesis story of Joseph and his brothers. *Eretz Gosen* (Land of Goshen) was given to the Hebrews by Joseph's pharaoh (Genesis 45:9–10). Abraham also passed through this part of Egypt when he fled there with Sarah (Genesis 12:10). There are archeological finds indicating the Hebrews, or Semites, lived in Goshen during this period and that they worshiped Yahweh. A wall painting dated to 1870 BCE in Egypt with text from Beni Hassan shows nomadic Semites entering Egypt along the "highway" leading through the Land of Goshen.[8]

An Austrian expedition led by Manfred Bietak found ruins of a "crowded, densely populated city with narrow streets and alleys and mud-brick construction" in the Goshen area. There is evidence of this city being occupied consistently for over 500 years, closely approximating the 430 years the Bible tells us the Hebrews lived there. There is also evidence of people used as slaves living at this site "making mud bricks for building, mining, working in the fields, and serving in households—just as we see various Israelites doing during their time in Egypt."[9]

Indirect evidence that the people of Goshen worshiped Yahweh has been discovered in Egyptian dynastic inscriptions and are the earliest references to a god named Yahweh found outside of the Bible.[6]

Tomb Images. Archeological evidence in support of the Bible story is found in images on Egyptian tombs of non-Egyptian foreign slaves making bricks. These images date from the time of the Exodus in 1446 BC.[6]

Hebrews in Egypt. "As for evidence that is more specific to the Israelites, the Brooklyn Papyrus lists almost 30 slaves with northwest Semitic names, several which are even Hebrew." This document is among the oldest (450 BCE) preserved writings about snake, scorpion, and spider bites. The papyrus is at New York's Brooklyn Museum.[10]

Evidence of Plagues. A Christian archaeologist, William F. Albright, has espoused what he believes to be historical evidence of the plagues. He has written that the biblical accounts are essentially correct. One example is the discovery at El Arish of an ancient water trough with hieroglyphics telling of a time of darkness.[11] However, Albright's work has been challenged by more modern archeologists.

There is one more aspect of these plagues that begs our attention. That is the orderly progression in the severity of the plagues which start with an environmental problem and move to human deaths. This progression provides evidence of planning, over against just natural occurrences. Otherwise, a random order would hardly provide the escalation of severity designed to put increasing pressure on the Egyptian rulers.

CONCLUSION

There are people who require absolute objectivity. This is not necessarily a bad thing especially when it concerns new medications and treatments for disease. People of faith are not oblivious to science, which can indeed explain much of what we see in this world. However, the eyes of faith "…are fixed, not on the things that are seen, but on the things that are unseen: for what is seen passes away; what is unseen is eternal" (II Corinthians 4:18). While many of the causes for plagues can be explained, the reason for the Egyptian rulers to free Hebrew slaves numbering more than 600,000 is more difficult. We must ask "Why would an economy dependent on the free work of slaves decide to let them all go especially in a time of great difficulty?" If the plagues can be explained by natural events, it is still exceptionally convenient that they occurred in the time frame and in the order that they were reported in the Bible.

If these Exodus passages were the only history, we have teaching us that God can perform powerful and life changing events, then we might be tempted to believe in more natural explanations. But we remember the most astonishing miracle of all—the resurrection. The God who can defeat death can easily have power over other natural events.

What have we learned about God from studying the miracles? God cares about His people; is sovereign over history and nature; is personal, powerful, and present; and provides what we need. He is mysterious and is persistent, among many other characteristics. We can understand many of these parts of who God is but others are simply to be accepted on faith.

REFERENCES

1. Sohma, M. (2016 November). Does the Ipuwer Papyrus provide evidence for the events of the Exodus? *Ancient Origins*,13, 49. Retrieved from http://www.ancient-origins.net/artifacts-ancient-writings/does-ipuwer-paprus-provide-evidence-events-exodus-006951.
2. Estes, A.C. (2013 March 3). With Passover approaching, a plague of locusts descends upon Egypt. *The Atlantic*. Retrieved from http://www.theatlantic.com/international/archive/2013/passover-approaching-plague-locusts-descends-upon-egypt/317767.
3. Gordon, T.J. (1966). Ideas in conflict. *The Miracles of Exodus.* New York: St. Martin's Press, pp. 18–48.
4. Kupferschmidt, K. (2018 August 17). Researcher at the center of an epic fraud remains an enigma to those who exposed him. *Science*. Retrieved from https://www.sciencemag.org/news/2018/08/researcher-center-epic-fraud-remains-enigma-those-who-exposed-him
5. Editorial, (2017 March 7). Science journalism can be evidence-based, compelling—and wrong. *Nature,* 543, 7644. Retrieved from

http://www.nature.com/news/science-journalism-can-be-evidence-based-compelling-and-wrong-1.21591.
6. Bohstron. P. (2016 April 14). Were Hebrews ever slaves in ancient Egypt? Yes. *HAARATZ*. Retrieved from https://www.haaretz.com/archaeology/were-hebrews-ever-slaves-in-ancient-egypt-yes-1.5429843.
7. Dever, W. (1996). Biblical archaeology review interviewing William Dever: Is this man a biblical archaeologist? Part I. *Biblical Archaeology Review,* 22(4):30-39ff.
8. _____. (2010). Patriarchs. *All About...Archaeology.* Retrieved from https://www.allaboutarchaeology.org/patriarchs.htm..
9. _____. (2002). Goshen. *All About...Archaeology.* Retrieved from https://www.allaboutarchaeology.org/goshen.htm.
10. Marry, A. (2004 January 21). The Brooklin papyrus. *Ancient Egyptian medical papyri*. Retrieved from *"Ancient Egyptian Medical Papyri"*.
11. Giuliani, C. (2009). *An alternative view of the distant past.* Morrisville, North Carolina: Lulu publishing. Retrieved from https://books.google.com/books?id=7ERyDwAAQBAJ&pg=PA294&lpg=PA294&dq=william+f+albright+el+arish+egypt&source=bl&ots=enn7CYgUHH&sig=ACfU3U2CakFrz_KzIW5LeLuAjC4_jYJb7g&hl=en&sa=X&ved=2ahUKEwjF7tjBqtXgAhVJMd8KHdrDAokQ6AEwA3oECAcQAQ#v=onepage&q=william%20f%20albright%20el%20arish%20egypt&f=false

CHAPTER 7   LEADER'S GUIDE: PLAGUES AND DELIVERY
EXODUS 7–12

PRELIMINARY THOUGHTS

There are many opinions about the dates of the Exodus story, and the scientific versus miraculous events of the delivery from Egyptian slavery. There are archeologists and historians who support the events recorded in Scripture, and there are those who do not. These Bible passages should be read with the goal of discovering more about God rather than proving when or how something happened in biblical history.

Exercise 1: Have someone in the group read Exodus 7:17–25.

MIRACLES PERFORMED FOR PHARAOH'S BENEFIT

Plague One: Blood in the Nile Water

Does belief in God's use of natural phenomena lessen our faith or strengthen it? Further exploration of this question might include whether belief in medical science to cure some diseases means God is not in the equation of healing, or whether God has provided the ability to heal as part of His created world.

Plagues Two, Three, Four, and Five: Frogs, Gnats, Flies, Disease

Exercise 2: Have someone in the group read Exodus 8 through 9:1–7.

Regarding the dating of the *Ipuwer Papyrus*, ask if there a scholar in the group who might address the slow evolution of any science versus the absolute belief in discoveries as they occur?

Exercise 3: For those of us who love animals and see them as innocent victims, this plague is difficult to understand. Of course, many of God's actions are difficult for humans to understand. Discuss why this approach would have impressed the Egyptian people with the power of the Hebrew God.

Did the Egyptian people know what Moses was telling Pharaoh? There was no Facebook during that time! Perhaps this visual image of seeing dead cattle versus live cattle would let the ordinary people know that God was at work in their world, and impress them with God's power.

Ask if they ever think about the sufferings of animals?

Plagues Six, Seven, and Eight: Festering Boils, Flashing Hail, and Locusts

Exercise 4: Have the group discuss this apparent discrepancy in Scripture.

A careful reading between Exodus 9:5–6 when all the beasts died, and Exodus 9:8–13 will show that no specific time frame is provided. Some plagues were said to follow the next day. But we should not assume that every plague followed on a daily basis. Something occurred between these plagues to allow the Egyptians to acquire more service animals.

Exercise 5: How are those who have put eternal trust in Jesus to process this information? We may wonder why God would turn someone against Him if indeed God did this. What do you think about this passage? Is there any emotion or feeling that you believe God caused you to have?

Let them explore this. It is difficult to reconcile the freedom we have to choose or reject faith, with the idea that God can manage our feelings. This is about God deliberately hardening the heart of a human. Perhaps there are those of us who need to be pushed through divine punishment into a place where God becomes our refuge. We have heard the expression that sometimes we must reach rock bottom to realize we need help. Can you share a personal experience here?

Another thread to pull here is to ask if a feeling of compassion for someone or some group develops over time. Perhaps an initial reaction to another's situation is apathy, but a second glance leads to a need to help.

MIRACLES PERFORMED TO SHOW GOD'S POWER OVER THE GODS OF EGYPT

Plague Nine: Impenetrable Darkness

Exercise 6: Have someone in the group read Exodus 12:1–5. What characteristic of God stands out to you in these verses?

Plague Ten: The Final Plague

God tells us to be mindful of our neighbor's needs and to share with him/her.

Exercise 7: Have someone read Exodus 12:12.

Exercise 8: What does the group know about the modern-day celebration of Passover? If you have Jewish friends as many of us do, do you ever participate in the Passover rituals?

Does anyone in the group have a problem with participating in a Jewish ritual? Remind them that the Old Testament is part of Christianity's Holy Bible. Our faith grew out of the Jewish faith, and the Son of God we worship was born into a Jewish family.

There is a ritual feast—the Seder—that is a main event of Passover. This feast takes place on the first night of Passover. There are multiple steps involved in the ritual feast provided in the *Haggaddah*.[1] The Seder may occur at home with family and friends, or in the broader community.

The cattle death problem rears its head again here.

Exercise 9: Have the group discuss this second discrepancy.

Exercise 10: Have someone in the group read Exodus 12:1–5. What characteristic of God stands out to you in these verses?

God is concerned about the poor who do not have a lamb to kill.

Exercise 11: Why did God give such explicit instructions for how to prepare and eat the sacrificial lambs?

The people are to thoroughly cook the sacrificial lamb which they will eat. Remember this was written prior to the discovery of the Germ Theory of Disease! But the God who knows this "theory" has given explicit instructions! The people are not to be wasteful but to eat that which was sacrificed to God. And they are to be prepared to leave—sandals on, dressed, and ready to go.

Exercise 12: Have someone read Exodus 12:34–36. What does it mean that the Hebrews were to ask their Egyptian neighbors for the items listed in these verses?

Later, in the wilderness journey, the people use gold and silver to do something special. We will study that in the Wilderness chapter. God knows the future and prepares us for what will come.

DID THE MIRACLES REALLY HAPPEN?

SUPPORT FOR THE EXODUS MATERIAL

After the group has fully discussed the support material, revisit the characteristics of God identified in Table 7. Does the group agree, disagree, or have any to add?

REVIEW THE CENTRAL THEME AND QUESTION.

Central theme of this lesson: The all-powerful God intervenes in history when it is part of His sacred design for humanity's good.

Central Question of this lesson: Were the lessons learned from events in Egypt specific only to history or can they apply to our lives today?

REFERENCE

1. _____. (n.d.). *English Haggadah text with instructional guide.* Brooklyn, NY: Kehot Publications Society. Retrieved from https://www.chabad.org/holidays/passover/pesach_cdo/aid/661624/jewish/English-Haggadah.htm

CHAPTER 8   MIRACLES IN THE WILDERNESS
EXODUS 14–24

Table 8: Characteristics of God Found in the Wilderness Experience

Characteristic	References	Characteristic	References
Will fight for us	Exodus 14:14	Can be annoyed	Exodus 14: 15–31
Knows His people and His creation	Exodus 13:17–18 Exodus 17:1–7	Values freedom	Exodus 13:21–22
Requires respect	Ecclesiastes 12:13	Speaks with us	Exodus 19:3–6
Deserves "Glory"	Exodus 14:18 John 11:4 Revelation 4:11	Provides physical nourishment	Exodus 15:22–25 Exodus 17:1–7
Is Sovereign over nature	Exodus 13:21–22 Exodus 14:26–29	Wants to provide healing	Exodus 15:26
Knows how we are made	Exodus 17:5–7	Cares about our safety	Exodus 14:19–20 Exodus 19:21
Can appear in nature	Exodus 13:21–22	Teaches us how to live	Exodus 20
Values physical rest	Exodus 16:4–5	Can sometimes be seen by humans	Exodus 24:9–11
Knows our needs	Exodus 15:22–25 Exodus 16:4–5	Leads and protects	Exodus 13:21–22 Exodus 14:19–20

Central Theme of this lesson: God continues to care for His people through many episodes of disobedience.

Central Question of this lesson: If God uses the created world's resources to help His people, is it still a miracle?

PRELIMINARY THOUGHTS

The miraculous occurrences did not stop with the plagues, nor when God delivered the Hebrew people across the waters. For 40 years God allowed them to wander in a wilderness, but He remained with them throughout the entire experience assisting when they needed help. God's faithfulness is again demonstrated through an extended timeline of caring.

THE GOD OF BATTLE

Exercise 1: "The Lord will fight for you; so hold your peace" (Exodus 14:14). What does this mean to our world today? Can we extrapolate the meaning to our own lives, or is this just about the situation in which Moses and the Hebrews found themselves?

<u>**God will fight for us**</u>. This particular passage is specifically about the Hebrews escaping from slavery, and from the Egyptians who are in hot pursuit. In Exodus and Deuteronomy there are many more references to battle than the one quoted above. For example, read Deuteronomy 20:1–9. According to one website, there are 59 references to battles in the Bible.[1] Not all of these references are assurances that God will be with the Hebrews but many are.

Exercise 2: Does God's command of "…hold your peace" apply only to large groups of people, or does it apply to individuals as well? To what extent do you internalize biblical historical messages into your life?

Even though Bible stories are often about specific events, we can glean lessons that help us live better lives. Perhaps the battles God fights for us are both corporate and individual, physical and spiritual. One example of how God fights for us in modern times came through the true story of a woman who underwent treatment for stomach cancer, and was hospitalized for more than 50 days. During her hospitalization, she received chemotherapy every few days through intravenous fluids. She would lay in her bed, look up at the IV bottle, and remember the first part of a verse from Isaiah (43:2a). **"When you pass through the waters, I will be with you…" She was assured that the IV "waters" were blessed by God. After treatment, she always had a high fever. Then she relied on the other part of the same verse for comfort: "…when you walk through the fire, you shall not be burned, nor shall the flame scorch you"** (43:2b). She was very comforted by this verse, and now, years later, she continues to rely on God's protection in battles.[2]

WADE IN THE WATER, CHILDREN

The final miracle performed by God in the deliverance of the Hebrews from Egypt was the parting of the waters that the Hebrews were able to walk through. Controversy about this miracle has most to do with exactly where the crossing of water could have occurred. "The Israelites set out from Rameses on the way to Succoth…" (Exodus 12:37a). Maps of ancient Egypt indicate there were two different cities named Succoth. One was near both the land of Goshen and Rameses—in the north of Egypt. The route through this Succoth would have required the people to cross a land mass involving lakes at the edge of Goshen. The lakes teemed with papyrus reeds—the Reed Sea—some of which were connected by canals. Three ancient sources—the *Teaching for*

Merikare, the relief map of Hatshepsut's Punt expedition, and the relief map of Seti I at Karnak—provide evidence of these canals which seemed designed to protect from invasion and to keep slaves from escaping eastward.[3] However, proof of the existence of the canals is not proof that this is where the Hebrews crossed.

The second Succoth location was on the Sinai Peninsula located at the end of the Gulf of Aqaba at the tip of the Sinai Peninsula. This route would have required the Hebrews to cross both the Sea of Reeds and the much wider Straits of Tiran. Either journey would have required crossing of waters by six hundred thousand men, and their dependents (Exodus 12:37).

Exercise 3: Have someone read Exodus 13:17–18.

God knows His people. The verses that make us think the longer route to the Straits of Tiran was taken are those from Exercise 3 above. God guided the Hebrews in the long way to Palestine, rather than by the shorter route. We cannot know God's reasons for selecting the longer, more difficult route. It could have been because the Hebrew people would have a harder time returning to their slavery if they changed their minds about escaping.

Exercise 4: Have you ever been faced with something so difficult that you were tempted to take the easier path or to stay in your particular rut? What decision did you finally make?

God values freedom for humans. The longer route is supported by the need for the Hebrews to depend on God to deliver them. Since the Hebrews lived near the shorter route—Goshen, they would have known that way. The longer route required them to put their faith in God to guide them. The Bible says that the Lord led them in the daytime in the form of a pillar of cloud and at night as a pillar of fire (theophany) so they could travel continuously (Exodus 13:21–22). This is another miraculous occurrence associated with the deliverance to freedom.

There was a need to move rapidly in order to escape a ruler who had gone back on his word many times. Exodus 14:9 has the pursuing Egyptians catch up with the Hebrews where they had encamped near a specific place—Pi-hahiroth to the east of Baal-xephron. These landmarks are located at the tip of the Sinai Peninsula. At this point, Moses had gained confidence in himself and in God throughout the series of miracles, and told his people to not be afraid and to stand still (Exodus 14:13).

Exercise 5: Have someone read Exodus 14:15–31. Have the group discuss the characteristics of God found in these verses.

<u>**God can be annoyed**</u>. When the Hebrews saw the army of Pharaoh, they panicked. God took Moses to task for this. The people had seen multiple miracles by God on their behalf yet they were terrified when the Egyptians appeared on the horizon. They grumbled at Moses that they had rather be slaves than die here.

Exercise 6: What does it take for us to believe and trust in God? Does it require one miracle—the resurrection, for example? Or does faith easily slip away when difficulties arise?

<u>**God deserves "Glory"**</u>**.** Exodus 14:18 tells us that God would win glory at the expense of the Egyptians. So why does God require Glory? At first blush we may think this is a bit high handed or even narcissistic. We think this because humans who demand glory often turn out to be despots, or have mental illness. But God is wholly Other, not human, not to be judged by a mirror reflection of humans, and definitely not subjected to the weaknesses that bother us. Imagine if a human had the power to create a universe! That human would quickly become completely besotted by power. But God continues to be the essence of Love, and is deserving of eternal adoration.

Dr. John Piper, American Calvinist Baptist pastor and chancellor of Bethlehem College and Seminary in Minneapolis, Minnesota, teaches that God's need for glory is the "essence of His love to us…God's love labors and suffers to break our bondage to the idol of self and focus our affections on the treasure of God."[4] Humans tend to consider love as it applies to themselves—who loves them or who they love. Jesus taught us there is someone outside of ourselves who is deserving of our devotion. He showed that love is doing anything needed, even dying on a cross, to point toward the glory of God.

Exercise 7: Can you think of a celebrity, a political figure, or a personal acquaintance who was not able to handle adoration in an appropriate manner? Have you ever wished for more power or more praise? If so, what motivated this wish?

Exercise 8: Is human praise always detrimental? Discuss the place of praise in the development of children. How often do you praise other adults and for what purpose usually?

There are many scriptural references to glory associated with God. In John 11:1–6 Jesus allows the death of Lazarus and only afterwards calls him from the tomb alive so that the miracle would bring glory to God (verse 4). "You are worthy, O Lord, to receive glory and honor and power; For You created all things, And by Your will they exist and were created" (Revelation 4:11).

Exercise 9: When do you feel closest to God? Does it involve praise of God? Do singing songs of praise affect your understanding of what it means to be more like Christ?

We hardly ever offer pure praise to God. Our praise is mostly associated with thanking God for something—healing, comfort, and other gifts. This may be because we lack real language for praise without gratitude associated with it.

Exercise 10: Have the group spend a few minutes in silent praise prayer. Then ask them to share how they phrased their praise in their minds.

God leads and protects us through the difficult times. The "angel of God" appears in these passages and is The Presence responsible for the cloud and the fire guiding the Hebrews on their way. When the Egyptians appeared, the cloud moved behind the escaping slaves as a protector and caused darkness to envelop the army. This allowed time for Moses to save them by stretching out his hand resulting in a strong wind parting the waters enough to allow passage for the Hebrew people.

God is sovereign over nature. The Hebrew people were on their march out of slavery when they encountered a body of water blocking escape. Egyptian soldiers were rapidly approaching behind. Then God used His power over nature to save them. If you read carefully, you will note that an east wind blew up all night and caused the waters to part (Exodus 14:21).

The reader may doubt this feat of nature. While rare, this does happen; Lake Erie can exhibit this phenomenon. "When a strong wind hits the long and narrow lake, an odd thing happens—the waters rise on one side some 16 feet higher than on the other, making it possible, if risky, to cross on the shallow side." "Carl Drews of the National Center for Atmospheric Research claims that a wind of about 63 mph would have been strong enough to push back the waters..."[5]

There is every reason to consider this an intervention from God even though there is also a scientific explanation. The wind happened at just the right time, in the right place, and lasted long enough for the Hebrew people to gain safety on the other side. Then the wind ceased, trapping the Egyptians and sweeping them out to sea. God is Lord of all creation.

NOT A DROP TO DRINK

Exercise 11: Read Exodus 15:22–27, and Exodus 17:2–6.

God knows our needs, both physical and spiritual. After three days of wandering in the wilderness, the people ran out of water and were thirsty. The waters at Marah were bitter, perhaps so salty the people could not drink. Then they started to murmur—something we can certainly understand when very thirsty. God intervened and told Moses to put a particular log into the waters. The waters became sweet so the people could drink.

God wants to provide healing. Literally speaking, this story is about another miracle where God meets the immediate needs of the people. But we can find a further application for our lives today: Following the episode at Marah, God led the people to Elim where we are told there were twelve springs and many palm trees to provide shade. The important application for us is that God can deliver us from the bitterness we encounter to a place of sweetness. God identifies Himself as the Healer (verse 26). God does not say, "for I am the one who turns bitter water into sweet water." Instead, God talks directly about our need for healing.

Exercise 12: Ask if anyone would like to share a personal story of deliverance from bitter to sweet.

God knows His creation. The stop at Rephidim again found the people without water to drink (Exodus 17:1-6). They were so thirsty, they began to blame Moses for freeing them, and even threatened to stone him. God instructed Moses to take elders of the community, go forward to a place named Horeb, and strike a rock with the staff Moses had used so effectively in Egypt.

Dr. Colin Humphreys, professor of materials science at Cambridge University and professor of experimental physics at the Royal Institution in London, notes that porous rocks like sandstone and limestone absorb so much water that "…when they are under ground we use them as aquifers, natural reservoirs of water." It is from limestone that caves and gorges are often made when the water carves out these cavities. Limestone can also be found as surface rock in some areas. Rephidim is near Mount Sinai, an area where there is much porous limestone.[6]

If the rocks were limestone containing water, this miracle is about the God who is present in our lives and cares for our needs through creation's resources. If the rocks were not those containing water, it is an even more impressive miracle. Either way, God's power is evident in how He provides for us.

Exercise 13: How do you feel about this explanation? Are you more comfortable believing there is nothing natural about miracles from God? Can you find

comfort in believing that God uses creation's resources to meet the needs of His people?

Exercise 14: Have you ever prayed for a miracle from God? If so, please share with the group what you wanted to happen, and the results and timing of the results.

<u>**God knows how we are made**</u>. Science notes that "in some organisms, up to 90% of their body weight comes from water. Up to 60% of the human adult male body is water." Even human bones contain some water.[7] God our creator knows this.

Exercise 15: Ask the group to think of other instances in the Bible when water was a prominent theme.

Water is a theme throughout the Bible. There are 800 references to water in the Old Testament alone.[8] The emphasis on water makes a great deal of sense when one remembers where the Hebrew people lived—in a dry, arid area of the world with scarce drinking water supply. Naturally, the people would focus significantly on water locations. The ruins of ancient communities (Tels) are located near water sources showing that people had to settle where they could find a supply of water.

BREAD AND BIRDS

<u>**God provides physical nourishment**</u>. Tucked between the water miracles in Exodus is the account of daily provision of food for the escaped slaves (Exodus 16:2–8). The Hebrews were complaining about being hungry when God told Moses how the people would be fed. The motherly characteristic of God concerned with nurturing our physical bodies provided bread in the morning and quail in the evening. The bread was made from a substance called "manna." Both the flock of quail, and the manna amount must have been huge to provide enough food for the 600,000 men, the female contingent, their slaves, and the children! The Hebrews had access to olives (Exodus 27:20) and spices (Exodus 30:22–23) for at least part of the journey. They also had cattle and sheep (Exodus 29:1)—enough to allow for sacrifices to be made (Exodus 29:36).

Additional references provide support for what God did during the 40 years of wilderness journey. The New Testament refers to the manna God provided. Jesus spoke of the manna that came from God, but did not prevent ultimate death. Jesus, however, offered living bread (John 6:30-58).

<u>**God values physical rest**</u>. The people were told to gather only enough manna for one day with one exception; the day before the Sabbath they were to gather two

day's supply of manna so they could rest on the Sabbath (Exodus 16:4-5). This timing is interesting in that the ten commandments have not yet been given to Moses, so there is not yet a formal commandment to remember to keep the Sabbath day holy. However, the first mention of a day of rest is found in the creation story when God rested on the seventh day. Perhaps the first humans followed this example and observed a weekly day of rest after exile from paradise.

FIRE AND CLOUDS

God speaks with humans. When the people reached the holy mountain—commonly thought to be Mt. Sinai, God spoke to Moses and told him to give a message to Israel. Perhaps the most beautifully poetic and reassuring part of this message is that God said, "I bore you on eagles' wings and brought you to myself." There are 33 references to eagles in the Bible, some not complimentary to the eagles. However, here we see God using the eagle to refer to deeds God has beautifully done. Some other eagle references include 2 Samuel 1:23, Isaiah 40:31, and Deuteronomy 32:11.

Exercise 16: Have someone read Exodus 19:9–25.

God can appear in nature. This was not the first time God appeared in fire and clouds. In Exodus 13:21–22, God led the Hebrew people by a cloud pillar during the day time, and by a pillar of fire at night. In the 19th chapter of Exodus, God again appeared as smoke and fire that settled over Mt. Sinai. God responded to Moses by way of thunder. Humphreys, a Christian professor of physics, explains his perspective on this as the eruption of a volcano.[6]

If it were indeed an erupting volcano, we can think about this in two ways—both of which show God's mighty power. (1) If Mt. Sinai were already an erupting volcano, this would mean the miracle is God's perfect timing to bring the people there, and of God's voice emerging from the eruption. (2) Or we can note that the timing and the voice remain confirmations that God is completely responsible for the eruption. However, Dr. Humphreys' theory is just one possibility for the events on Mount Sinai.

God cares about our safety. God spoke and told Moses to prevent the people from coming up the mountain; only Moses and Aaron were to approach. There could not be hundreds of thousands of people on an erupting volcano no matter how much they wanted to be near to God because "many of them will perish." In addition, one would imagine that more than a million people crowding around would not allow Moses to receive God's word in any accurate manner! Have you ever tried to quiet a crowd?!

Exercise 17: How do you feel about safety in the performance of God's work? Are we to proceed "headlong" into potential danger (rushing into the burning building or doing missionary work in a war-torn country)?

<u>**God teaches us how to live**</u>. At this point, God gave humanity the ten commandments. To study these, please see Chapter 10.

HOLY FEAR

Exercise 18: Have someone read Exodus 24:9–11.

<u>**God was seen by Moses and the Elders**</u>. This passage says that God appeared with feet standing on a pavement of sapphire, clear blue as the very heavens. Moses and the elders ate and drank before God. Moses went further up into the cloud on the mountain and stayed 40 days and 40 nights.

<u>**God requires our respect**</u>. There clearly are scriptures stating that we must fear God such as Ecclesiastes 12:13. The word "fear" may have a translation problem. Consider that the Exodus 20:20 verse—"Do not be afraid; for God has come only to test you and to put the fear of Him upon you so that you do not sin"—could easily mean that we must be in awe of God, and honor and respect our Lord. We do this for God just as we would do for a loving parent—honor, respect, love. This seems to be a mixed message. But if we read if through the lens of Love, we can conclude that we are not meant to be afraid. Rather we are meant to obey so that we can have a good life.

Exercise 19: Do you fear God? What are your feelings in this regard about God?

CONCLUSION

Miracles are clustered throughout the book of Exodus. Coupled with each miraculous occurrence is an indication of who God is and how much He loves His creation.

God was among us and continues to be among us—sometimes as fire and cloud, sometimes as provider of nourishment, and sometimes as One who commands awe. Fear and trust, perhaps two sides of one coin, are required of those who worship the God of Abraham and Sarah, of Isaac and Rebekah, of Jacob and Rachel, and of you.

REFERENCES

1. _____. (n.d.). Knowing Jesus. *Battles*. Retrieved from https://bible.knowing-jesus.com/topics/Battles.
2. Conversation with M. Harwood, (2017).
3. _____. (2018). All About Archaeology. *Goshen*. Retrieved from http://www.allaboutarchaeology.org/goshen.htm.
4. Piper, J. (2007). How is God's passion for His own glory not selfishness? *Desiring God*. Retrieved from http://www.desiringgod.org/articles/how-is-gods-passion-for-his-own-glory-not-selfishness.
5. Mooney, C. (2014, December 8). No, really: There is a scientific explanation for the parting of the Red Sea. *The Washington Post*, retrieved from http://www.biblicalpov.com/miracles-of-moses-in-exodus.html#sthash.rabjCS12.dpbs
6. Humphreys, C. (2005). Science and the miracles of Exodus. *Europhysics News* May/June. Vol. 36. N0.3 p.93-96. Retrieved from https://www.europhysicsnews.org/articles/epn/pdf/2005/03/epn05306.pdf.
7. Mitchell, H.H., Hamilton, T.S., Steggerda, R.H., Mitchell, T.S., & Bean H.W. (1945). The chemical composition of the adult human body and its bearing on the biochemistry of growth. *Journal of Biological Chemistry*, 158:625-637. Cited in the water in you. *USGS*. Retrieved from https://water.usgs.gov/edu/propertyyou.html.
8. Finger, R.H. (2013). A river runs through it. *Sojourners*. Retrieved from https://sojo.net/magazine/november-2013/river-runs-through-it#node-50597.

CHAPTER 8   LEADER'S GUIDE: MIRACLES IN THE WILDERNESS
EXODUS 14–24

PRELIMINARY THOUGHTS

This is the final chapter involving the life of Moses. Here we learn of his commitment to leading God's Covenant people through the wilderness in spite of their murmuring and disobedience.

Discuss exercises 1 and 2 together

THE GOD OF BATTLE

Exercise 1: "The Lord will fight for you; so hold your peace" (Exodus 14:14). What does this mean to our world today? Can we extrapolate the meaning to our own lives, or is this just about the situation in which Moses and the Hebrews found themselves?

Exercise 2: Does God's command "…hold your peace" apply only to large groups of people, or does it apply to individuals? To what extent do you internalize biblical historical messages into your life?

If today's newspapers are to be believed, communities, families, and personal lives are filled with violence. Even in families there are cases of severe disruption and murder. Already we have encountered a biblical story of a murdered brother. Does every verse in the Bible hold a message for us today, or are some stories simply about the historical events?

How difficult is it for you to "Hold Your Peace" in daily life? In family life?

WADE IN THE WATER, CHILDREN

Exercise 3: Have someone read Exodus 13:17–18.

Exercise 4: Have you ever been faced with something so difficult that you were tempted to take the easier path or to stay in your particular rut   What decision did you finally make?

Give the group a chance to share but don't belabor this question.

Exercise 5: Have someone read Exodus 14:15–31. Have the group discuss the characteristics of God found in these verses.

The leader may want to list these on a board as the discussion proceeds.

Exercise 6: What does it take for us to believe and trust in God? Does it require one miracle—the resurrection, for example? Or does faith easily slip away when difficulties arise?

Has anyone in the group experienced a miraculous event?

Exercise 7: Can you think of a celebrity, a political figure, or a personal acquaintance who was not able to handle adoration in an appropriate manner? Have you ever wished for more power or more praise? If so, what motivated this wish?

As you lead the group, remember that not all desire for more power is evil. For example, a spouse who is abused may wish for the power to leave the relationship.

Exercise 8: Is human praise always detrimental? Discuss the place of praise in the development of children. How often do you praise other adults and for what purpose usually?

When parents' struggle to put food on the table sometimes holding 2 or 3 jobs, it may preclude time for frequent demonstrations of love for each other and for their children. Did your parents tell you they loved you? Do you praise your own children? How should praise of children be handled in order to encourage self-esteem?

Exercise 9: When do you feel closest to God? Does it involve praise of God? Do singing songs of praise affect your understanding of what it means to be more like Christ?

Is there a difference among the group's composition concerning those who find it easy to praise God but difficult to praise other people?

Exercise 10: Have the group spend a few minutes in silent praise prayer. Then ask them to share how they phrased their praise in their minds.

NOT A DROP TO DRINK

Exercise 11: Read Exodus 15:22–27, and Exodus 17:2–6.

Exercise 12: Ask if anyone would like to share a personal story of deliverance from bitter to sweet.

Exercise 13: How do you feel about this explanation? Are you more comfortable believing there is nothing natural about miracles from God? Can you find comfort in believing that God uses creation's resources to meet the needs of His people?

Let the group explore their beliefs without judgment.

Exercise 14: Have you ever prayed for a miracle from God? If so, please share with the group what you wanted to happen, and the results and timing of the results.

Exercise 15: Ask the group to think of other instances in the Bible when water was a prominent theme.

Baptism comes to mind. Use of the Jordan River waters for healing is another instance. Think of the man who waited patiently by the waters in Jerusalem but could never make it into the pool in time. Are there waters today that are seen as healing? One might think of President Roosevelt and Hot Springs.

BREAD AND BIRDS

Exercise 16: Have someone read Exodus 19:9–25.

Exercise 17: How do you feel about safety in the performance of God's work? Are we to proceed "headlong" into potential danger (rushing into the burning building or doing missionary work in a war-torn country)?

Ask them how they would feel if their grown child felt called to go to Syria to preach the Gospel, or to South Sudan to provide medical care?

HOLY FEAR

Exercise 18: Have someone read Exodus 24:9–11.

Exercise 19: Do you fear God? What are your feelings in this regard about God?

Did you fear your parents while growing up? Or your teachers? What caused you to fear a person in authority over you when you were young?

CONCLUSION

Review the characteristics of God identified in this judgment session. Does the class agree with these? Are there additions to be listed?

REVISIT THE CENTRAL THEME AND QUESTION.

Central Theme of this lesson: God continues to care for His people through many episodes of disobedience.

Central Question of this lesson: If God uses His created world's resources to help people, is it still a miracle?

CHAPTER 9   FIRE AND CLOUDS
EXODUS 20, 32, 33, 38, 40

Table 9: Characteristics of God Found in Signs of His Presence

Characteristic	References	Characteristic	References
Chooses Us as Individuals	Exodus 31:1–2	Experiences Anger	Exodus 32:10
Responds to Our Pleas	Exodus 32:14 Exodus 32:12 Jonah 3:8–10	Gives Special Gifts	Isaiah 11:2 Romans 12:6–15 I Corinthians 12:7–11
Makes His Presence Known	Exodus 40:34–38	Not Bound by Tradition	Matthew 12
His Patience Has a Limit	Exodus 33:1–6	Has Amazing Patience	John 18:13–27
Provides Our Needs	I Samuel 21:6	Is Mysterious	1 Corinthians 13:12
Cares for Our Wellbeing	Isaiah 4: 5–6	Provides Signs of His Greatness	Exodus 14:24
Cares about the details of our lives	Exodus 16:5		

Central Theme for this lesson: What we know of God is what He has chosen to reveal to us.

Central Question for this lesson: Do these stories have anything to do with me today?

PRELIMINARY THOUGHTS

Exodus has many important stories with the ability to convey essential truths for the living of our lives. There are chapters concerned with such things as the building of altars of earth or stones, the Tent of the Presence, and gold-plated articles to be placed in the Tent. The book also has details of what NOT to construct such as gods of silver to be worshipped (Exodus 20:22–26). We study these stories in order to learn more about the God we worship.

SPIRITUAL GIFTS

<u>God chooses us as individuals</u>. Exodus 31:1-2 tells us of a particular man, Bezalel son of Uri, who experienced a call.

Exercise 1: We have studied that God chose the Hebrew people, the descendants of Abraham, to be His people and to inherit the land of Canaan. In this passage, we find that God chooses individuals as well. Have you ever felt chosen by God?

<u>God gives special gifts</u>. An Old Testament passage (Isaiah 11:2) lists spiritual gifts as wisdom, understanding, counsel, might, knowledge, fear of the Lord. The New

Testament provides additional lists of spiritual gifts such as prophecy, ministry, teaching, exhorting, generosity, diligence, cheerfulness (Romans 12: 6–15).

Exercise 2: A lot of different gifts have been listed and there are more Biblical references about gifts given by God (I Corinthians 12: 7–11). What do you conclude about God's gifts to us? Do you believe you have received one or more spiritual gifts?

GOD TAKES OUR PRAYERS SERIOUSLY

Exercise 3: Have someone read Exodus 32:7–14.

It was in chapter 24 that God told Moses to return to the mountain. Moses stayed there through chapter 32. We do not know the exact time spent with God on the mountain. However, it was so long that the people grew anxious and decided they needed another "god" to take care of them; they persuaded Aaron to cast a golden calf for their worship.

God experiences anger. These Hebrew people abandoned their God even though they had experienced many miracles while being delivered from Egyptian slavery. Granted, it had been 40 years since the plagues in Egypt so they could have forgotten or been born after the escape. However, God had maintained His presence through fire and cloud, and by providing quails and manna. These people were either extremely anxious when left without Moses' leadership, or were totally without gratitude! God knew what they were doing down below the mountain and told Moses that "…my wrath may burn hot against them and I may consume them; and of you I will make a great nation" (Exodus 32:10).

God responds to our pleas. Moses began to plead with God to spare the people. He even made an argument worthy of a lawyer: Moses reminded God that the Egyptians would say, "It was with evil intent that he brought them out to kill them in the mountains, and to consume them from the face of the earth" (Exodus 32:12). "The Lord changed his mind about the disaster that he planned to bring on his people" (Exodus 32:14).

Exercise 4: Discuss the personal choice that Moses made when he pled with God to spare the people.

But wait just a minute! Malachi 3:6, and other scriptures, quote God as saying, "For I the Lord do not change." Let us explore what the passages just read in Exodus tell us about the God who sometimes says He is unchanging.

How we believe about whether God changes His mind or not depends on what we believe about how God interacts with us. The following perspectives repeated from Chapter 3 represent the belief systems we hold.

Exercise 5: Psalm 119:4 is another passage that reassures us of God's constancy. But there are other verses (Exodus 32:12 and Jonah 3:8–10) indicating that God can and does change His mind. Using the following four systems of belief, discuss what you think about the Exodus 32:12 passage.

(1) If we are **Calvinists** then our belief is that there is no need for God to really change since He already knows and determines everything that we will do and that will happen.
(2) There is no need for God to change in **Arminianism** either since this belief system asserts that while God gives us freedom, He already knows what will happen.
(3) **Open theism** teaches that the future is open for God as it is for us. So here, God would allow us to change His mind about things through our prayers and pleas to Him; He has made His plans for us conditional on our actions.
(4) In **process theology**, the belief is that the future is not set for us or for God. The most obvious example is that God experienced incarnation for the first time when Jesus was sent into the world.[1]

GOD'S PATIENCE

God's patience has a limit. During the wilderness journeys, God tolerated many acts of defiance from the Hebrews and still remained faithful. However, in Exodus 33:1–6, God tells Moses, "I will not go up among you, or I would consume you on the way, for you are a stiff-necked people." Instead, God will send an angel to take them the rest of the way. God prevents himself from consuming the people by withdrawing.

God's patience is awesome. We have a previous story of God actually "blotting out" all the people on the globe with the exception of the righteous Noah and his family. However, do not fear since God seems to take a very long time to lose patience. God stayed with the Hebrews for the 40 years of their journey through the wilderness even after the episode of the golden calf. It was only at the very end as they approached the promised land when He backed away. Even then, He sent an angel to lead them onward. The New Testament provides more information about the patience of God—He went so far as to send a person of the trinity, Jesus the Christ, to die for our sins. In that situation, Jesus, with great patience, named Peter as the "rock" of the church even though Peter denied him three times at a very critical juncture.

God cannot be totally understood by His creation. So how are we to process these characteristics of God—mercy and anger? As human emotions, they seem contradictory. However, now we "see through a glass darkly" (KJV) or "see in a mirror dimly" (NRSV) and cannot know anything about the Creator God except what He reveals to us. This is where trust enters the picture. If we put our full trust in God, we will have the complete love and mercy of God with us. These are gifts freely given to those who ask, and they are awesome and unmatchable gifts when compared to anything we know or can know.

PLANNING AHEAD

Exercise 6: Have someone read Exodus 38:24–25.

  <u>**God is the God of history**</u>. This chapter and the following in Exodus are about the completion of the Tent of the Presence where the Ark of the Covenant was to be kept. Many verses talk about forming articles out of gold and silver.

Exercise 7: Where did the Hebrews get this gold and silver?

SACRED BREAD

Exercise 8: Have someone read Exodus 40:22–23 and Numbers 4:7–8

  <u>**God provides for our physical needs**</u>. In Matthew 12:3–4, Jesus told the story of David and his men being given sacred bread to eat when they were hungry (I Samuel 21:6). In this Samuel story, the day-old sacred bread was all that was available. The day-old sacred bread was meant strictly for the priests, and was so special that only the Levites could even look at it (Numbers 4). But God allowed it to be repurposed when people were hungry.

  <u>**God is ever present in our lives**</u>. Bread is a recurring theme throughout the Bible. When the people were enslaved, unleavened bread allowed them to escape quickly. When we wander about in whatever wilderness of sin we find ourselves, God will provide spiritual sustenance. When we are hungry of body or spirit, God repurposes sacred matters in order to feed us. And, most importantly, Jesus suffered and died that we might find salvation—symbolized by the broken bread. The point of all the bread stories seems to be how much we are loved.

Exercise 9: Why was it important to God to keep bread always in the sacred Tent (Exodus 25:30)? Can you think of a New Testament quote involving bread?

  <u>**God is not bound by tradition**</u>. Traditions were an important part of ancient life. Traditions associated with the Sabbath included the gathering and preparation of manna by the Israelites; they were not to gather or prepare the food on the holy day (Exodus 16:5). Sabbath traditions were taken so seriously that one man who gathered sticks on the Sabbath was stoned to death for this act (Numbers 15:32–36). Although gathering grain was against the traditions of Torah Judaism, Jesus' disciples did just that, and Jesus defended them (Matthew 12).

Exercise 10: Numbers 15:35–40 tells us that it was God who told the people to stone the man who gathered sticks on the holy day. How can we square this with what Jesus did and taught on the Sabbath? Reading further in verses 36–40 may provide guidance as to why the man was punished.

God cares about the details of our lives. Rituals, from the most formal to everyday small performances, provide us with a sense of the appropriate. Some small rituals are helpful in everyday life. As an example, the appropriate choice of an eating utensil is usually well-known in every society—we do not have to waste time deciding among fork, chopsticks, or fingers before every meal. Rituals provide security and comfort as we live our lives. God gave His people rituals to follow even when they were lost in wilderness. But when the need arose, exceptions were always made to show God's mercy.

SACRED TEXTS

Exercise 11: What are we to make of this? Is the New Testament more legitimate than the Old? We know that Jesus sometimes quoted the Old Testament. Jesus said he did not come to destroy the law but to fulfill it. Neither he nor his disciples had the New Testament to guide them.

It was around the middle of the second century CE that Christians began to see the need for a permanent record of the events in the life of Jesus. Hence, the New Testament was pulled together from the letters and Gospels into one "book". The stance the Christian Church has taken since that time is that both testaments are sacred writings.

> That which was used by the Redeemer himself for the sustenance of his own soul can never pass out of the use of his redeemed. That from which he proved the divinity of his mission and the age-long preparation for his coming must always have a principal place in his Church's argument for him.[2]

Exercise 12: Have someone read II Timothy 3:15–17.

This passage in Timothy sheds light on two important points. The first is that the Scriptures we have are sufficient for our salvation. And the second point is that these words were never meant to provide scientific explanations. Rather they were and are meant for the righteousness of our souls, that we may be morally perfected for the glory of God, and that we may take on "every good work." "Any theory of the Old Testament which makes no distinction between scientific and historical statements on the one hand, and religious and ethical statements on the other, is inadequate and erroneous, because it is not in accord with the New Testament teaching on that point."[3]

The argument that some put forth regarding the incorrect science found in some parts of the Bible is a bogus argument when used to disprove the veracity of Scripture. We do not need to search the Biblical texts to find how to explain the atom. "Philosophy and science have not always been friendly toward the idea of God, the reason being that they are dedicated to the task of accounting for things and are impatient with anything that refuses to give an account of itself."[4]

Jesus said he did not come to destroy the law but to fulfill it. Neither he nor his disciples had what we call the New Testament to guide them. Jesus himself provided guidance for the use of the Old Testament. He fed hungry people and healed sick people on the holy Sabbath in spite of restrictions placed on Sabbath day activity. He did this because of the second greatest commandment, to love neighbors as we love ourselves. He did this because God has shown time and time again even in just the first two books of the Bible, that He loves His creation, shows mercy, and desires our happiness.

The writer of Hebrews provides insight into how early Christians viewed the Old Testament (chapter 1:1–2). In these verses, we learn that God spoke to humans in different methods, and amounts over many centuries, but then provided us with a fuller account through Jesus Christ, the second person of the Trinity.

THE PRESENCE OF GOD

God makes His presence known in wondrous ways. "Whenever the cloud was taken up, the Israelites would set out on each stage of their journey; but if the cloud was not taken up, then they did not set out until the day that it was taken up (Exodus 40:36–37).

Exercise 13: Can you think of reasons why the God who loves us would delay the people at times, and at other times send them on their way?

God cares for His creation's wellbeing. This is not the first time a cloud has been used by God to help His people. In earlier passages we learned that the Israelites marched both day and night, hence the need for smoke in the daytime, and fire at night. Marching at night makes sense based on the experiences of modern archeological expeditions in the Middle East. These expeditions start to dig before the break of day, and finish before the hottest part of the day to avoid the extreme midday desert heat. Isaiah 4:5–6 provides more evidence for this interpretation: "…the Lord will create a cloud of smoke by day and a bright flame of fire by night; for glory shall be spread over all as a covering and a canopy, a shade from the heat by day, a refuge and a shelter from rain and tempest."

God provides signs of His greatness. Imagine if this cloud and fire could be seen by other people groups such as Nomads travelling in the wilderness at the same time as the Hebrews! These ancient days were times of superstitions and fears of natural processes. The signs of God's presence were protective, not harmful like a tornado might be. But the cloud and fire also showed the power of God to the enemies of the Hebrews; the Egyptians were panicked by signs of God's presence (Exodus 14:24). Therefore, we may assume the fire and cloud provided a witness to others of God's protective gift, and a warning to let the people go.

CONCLUSION

In modern times we may have trouble relating to some of the biblical materials. We seldom encounter miracles of nature such as guidance by clouds and fire. However, other stories can resonate strongly in our lives: We often negotiate with God to save a dear one who has cancer; we incorporate sacred bread into our worship as Jesus commanded us to do; we hope to strengthen our spiritual gifts and to recognize them in others; and we study both Testaments and hold them to be the inspired word of God.

God's plan has not been fully worked out in our world. So, we must not forget that miraculous signs in nature may still arise to show us the power of our God.

REFERENCES

1. Whitehead, A. N. (1929). *Process and reality. An essay in cosmology. Gifford lectures delivered in the University of Edinburgh during the session 1927–1928.* New York: Macmillan.
2. Smith, G.A. (1901). *Modern criticism and the preaching of the Old Testament.* New York: A.C. Armstrong and Co. p.19. Retrieved from http://biblehub.com/library/eiselen/the_christian_view_of_the_old_testament/chapter_i_the_new_testament.htm
3. Eiselen, C.F. (2015). *The Christian view of the Old Testament.* Retrieved from https://www.createspace.com/AboutUs.jsp.
4. Tozer, A.W. (1961). *Knowledge of the holy.* Retrieved from http://www.ntcg-aylesbury.org.uk/books/knowledge_of_the_holy.pdf, p.19.

CHAPTER 9   LEADER'S GUIDE: FIRE AND CLOUD
Exodus 20, 32, 33, 38, 40

PRELIMINARY THOUGHTS

These exercises involve many of the remaining items in Exodus that are not associated with any big particular biblical saga. Many people will not be familiar with them unless they are long-time biblical scholars.

SPIRITUAL GIFTS

Exercise 1: We have studied that God chose the Hebrew people, the descendants of Abraham, to be His people and to inherit the land of Canaan. In this passage, we find that God chooses individuals as well. Have you ever felt chosen by God?

Ask about their professions. Are they in careers in which they feel God has put them? Or perhaps they have a hobby that seems given by God such as making toys for kids or knitting shawls for homeless people.

Exercise 2: A lot of different gifts have been listed and there are more biblical references about gifts given by God (I Corinthians 12: 7–11). What do you conclude about God's gifts to us? Do you believe you have received one or more spiritual gifts?

Assure the class that it is OK for them to identify their gifts. No one should think of it as bragging since these come from God. Ask if they are using their spiritual gifts to the best of their ability. Let them identify better ways to use their own gifts. Let them identify the gifts of others in the class; perhaps there is one person who the class thinks speaks wisely, for example, or who has the gift of hospitality.

GOD TAKES OUR PRAYERS SERIOUSLY

Exercise 3: Have someone read Exodus 32:7–14.

Exercise 4: Discuss the personal choice that Moses made when he pled with God to spare the people.

Please note that God had said he would reward Moses by making of him a great nation. The response of Moses showed his integrity when he chose the people over his own glory, and over his own family. Ask them if they could choose others over their own family's future glory? Can they think of any decision in which one might choose to do something that might harm one's family? What about those young adults who decide to abandon their family and flee from a country where war is raging even though they know the family remaining will suffer because of the abandonment?

Exercise 5: Psalm 119:4 is another passage that reassures us of God's constancy. But there are other verses (Exodus 32:12 and Jonah 3:8–10) indicating that God can and does change His mind. Using the following four systems of belief, discuss what you think about the Exodus 32:12 passage.

Lead them as they reexplore the 4 ways theologians believe God interacts with us. No one has to believe in one or several but let them explore their options.

(1) If we are Calvinists then our belief is that there is no need for God to really change since He already knows and determines everything that we will do and that will happen. **Does this mean there is no need to pray because God has already decided everything? Yes – this is what it means**. These folks pray only for their personal growth in their relationship with God.

(2) There is no need for God to change His mind in Arminianism either since this belief system asserts that while God gives us freedom, He already knows what will happen. **Does this mean that God tricks us by pretending to change? No - God does not "trick" us—He has no need to do that since He is all powerful. It is simply a fact that God is both the Alpha and the Omega.**

(3) Open theism teaches that the future is open for God as it is for us. So here, God would allow us through our prayers and pleas to Him to change His mind about things; He has made His plans for us conditional on our actions. **Does this mean we have the ability to reject God? Yes – we have had that ability since tasting of the Tree of the Knowledge of Good and Evil.**

(4) In process theology, the belief is that the future is not set for us or for God. The most obvious example is that God experienced incarnation for the first time when Jesus was sent into the world. **Can we still trust God to guide our future if his future world is not set? Yes – remember all the other wonderful characteristics of God**.[1]

Summarize this exercise for them in the following way: God does change His attitude when we pray or when we change what we are doing. For example, the passage in Jeremiah 26:3 quotes God as saying that He will change His mind if the people change. However, **this does not mean that God changes His essence**. He is always just and merciful and loving; He is always the Alpha and the Omega—He is always eternal. We cannot say that God cannot change because by doing so we place our own limits on God. However, we cannot say that He often changes because this simply defies scripture. God's change is best understood by noting that the changes are in relationship to His creation, and not about His very being.

GOD'S PATIENCE

PLANNING AHEAD

Exercise 6: Have someone read Exodus 38:24–25.

Exercise 7: Where did the Hebrews get this gold and silver?

If no one in the class mentions what the Hebrew slaves were told by God to take from their neighbors when they fled Egypt, have them read Exodus 12:35–36.

SACRED BREAD

Exercise 8: Have someone read Exodus 40:22–23 and Numbers 4:7–8

Exercise 9: Why was it important to God to keep bread always in the sacred Tent (Exodus 25:30)? Can you think of a New Testament quote involving bread?

Was the bread on the Table for the Bread of the Presence (Exodus 25:23–30) a prelude to the Last Supper? Remind them that Jesus is the bread of life. Ask if they think this bread in the Tent foreshadowed Jesus' incarnation or was there another reason. We speak of "taking communion" when we observe the sacred ritual of the bread and wine. Communion refers to presence and community. Could this be God's purpose in focus on bread—that He is present with us?

Exercise 10: Numbers 15:35–40 tells us that it was God who told the people to stone the man who gathered sticks on the holy day. How can we square this with what Jesus did and taught on the Sabbath? Reading further in verses 36-40 may provide guidance as to why the man was punished.

It appears from these verses that God made the point that obedience to His commands was more important than life. Remember that these events occurred in a much more primitive time than ours. The Hebrew people had dangers in their environment and in the cultures around them that threatened to severely compromise their new relationship with God. The structure that God provided through His commandments grounded the people in a new, better, and safer way of life than they previously had.

SACRED TEXTS

Exercise 11: What are we to make of this? Is the New Testament more legitimate than the Old? We know that Jesus often quoted the Old Testament. Jesus said he did not come to destroy the law but to fulfill it. Neither he nor his disciples had the New Testament to guide them.

How do you think about the Old Testament? Do you usually dismiss it because it is the "Old" testament? During this study have you found new meaning in these ancient texts?

Help the group to understand that the New Testament reveals teachings that are more connected to Jesus who lived and walked among us. Jesus taught more by example than by obeying tradition. Jesus offered salvation and access to the Kingdom of God to everyone who simply believed rather than having to work to obey every law. This does not mean that the Old Testament has no meaning for us today. It has rich wisdom to enhance our lives, as it did for Jesus and his disciples.

Exercise 12: Have someone read II Timothy 3:15–17.

THE PRESENCE OF GOD

Exercise 13: Can you think of reasons why the God who loves us would delay the people at times, and at other times send them on their way?

Perhaps it was the heat of the land that God was concerned about. Or maybe the God of all Creation knew of dangers ahead to be avoided by waiting, or of the need the people might have to rest a little longer. Has anyone in the group ever felt that God had protected them from something bad by a fortuitous or even annoying delay in their planned day?

CONCLUSION

Review the identified characteristics of God in these passages. Does the class agree with these? Are there additions to be listed?

REVISIT THE CENTRAL THEME AND QUESTION.

Central Theme for this lesson: What we know of God is what He has chosen to reveal to us.

Central Question for this lesson: Do these stories have anything to do with me today?

REFERENCE

1. Whitehead, A.N. (1929). Process and reality. An essay in cosmology. *Gifford Lectures Delivered in the University of Edinburgh During the Session 1927–1928.* New York: Macmillan 1929.

CHAPTER 10 — THE COMMANDMENTS
EXODUS 20

Table 10: Characteristics of God Shown in the Ten Commandments

Characteristic	Reference	Characteristic	Reference
Worthy of Worship	Exodus 20:3 Deuteronomy 6:7	Desires Respect	Exodus 20:7
Commands Us	Exodus 20	Values All Life	Exodus 20:8–11 Exodus 20:13
Is a Living Being	Exodus 20:4–6	Rewards Obedience	Exodus 20:6 Exodus 20:12
Desires Faithfulness	Exodus 20:14	Jealous	Exodus 20:4–6
Values Justice	John 8:7 Exodus 20:16	Values Thoughts and Actions	Matthew 5:21–22 Exodus 20:17
Teaches How to Live	Exodus 20	Wants Us to Rely on Him	Exodus 20:4 and 5

Central Theme of this Lesson: God gave us instructions on how to live righteous lives.

Central Question of this Lesson: How am I to apply these ancient commandments in modern life?

PRELIMINARY THOUGHTS

The ten commandments were in the news in previous years especially in the states of Tennessee and Alabama. In Tennessee, the legislature tried unsuccessfully to pass a law that the commandments be displayed in all public buildings. In Alabama, a judge defied orders to remove a plaque of the commandments from his courtroom, and later responded to the court order by installing a huge stone monument of the ten commandments on the court grounds.

As you study what follows, consider the role that the ten commandments have in your life, and how important they are to you. Our purpose is to understand more about the God we worship through delving into the meaning and importance of the sacred commandments.

Exercise 1: How many of the ten commandants can the class remember?

Every Sunday School child has had to memorize the ten commandments at some time or another (Exodus 20:1–17). These ten encompass a range of subjects about the proper behavior of one who worships the Lord of Heaven and Earth. We will go through them one at a time in order to gain perspective on how to live in the modern world, and on what these particular rules tell us about God.

THE FOUR CATEGORIES OF COMMANDMENTS

The first four commandments in the Old Testament are about God and how we are to relate to the Creator. There follows a transition commandment leading into the laws about how individuals should conduct themselves. Finally, there is a commandment that applies to the inner life of us all.

In the New Testament, the greatest commandment is about loving the Lord with all heart, strength, and mind (Matthew 22:36-40)—an emphasis clearly underscoring that God should be foremost in our lives in the first four commandments.

Category One: The Place of God in Our Lives

Commandment Number One—**No Other Gods**

"You shall have no other gods before me" (Exodus 20:3; Deuteronomy 6:7).

God alone is worthy of worship. The Covenant people had a history of easily being dissuaded from the worship of the one true God. They were certainly very quick to ask Aaron to make something of metal that they could worship when Moses stayed on the mountain too long. It was only much later during the Babylonian exile that they seemed to "get it" for the first time and become the monotheistic people of the Bible.

There are scholars who think the fear ancient humans had about many aspects of life led them to seek protection from higher powers. Based on missionary stories, this fear remains true today for poor, rural communities in some underdeveloped countries. Fear is understandable in primitive times since humans are slow, furless creatures without defenses such as talons or fangs. The fear which originated the need for gods would also have caused people to fear the very "god" they hoped would save them; perhaps worship of manufactured gods was more about hoping bad things would not happen than it was about a god on whom one could depend.

God commands us. When the Creator God of Abraham, Isaac, and Jacob told us not to depend on "things" as gods, it was an act of love. Finally, we could rely on the living God who loves us! Finally, we could be free of fear! How wonderful is that?!

Exercise 2: What "gods" do we have before us today? Are you in danger of letting something take first place in your life over God such as social position or

patriotism? Or perhaps you place your family above all else? Has this commandment meant something special to you personally?

Commandment Number Two—No Images to Worship

You shall not make for yourself an idol, whether in the form of anything that is in heaven above, or that is on the earth beneath, or that is in the water under the earth. You shall not bow down to them or worship them; for I, the Lord your God, am a jealous god, punishing children for the iniquity of parents to the third and fourth generation of those who reject me, bu showing steadfast love to the thousandth generation of those who love me and keep my commandments (Exodus 20:4–6).

The actual commandment is longer than what we see carved on plaques or have memorized. It is a little frightening at one part, but ends in a wonderful reassurance.

God is a Living Being. Throughout history, humans worshiped whatever seemed at their disposal—gold, stone, and carvings. Some humans even declared themselves to be gods—such as the Pharaohs. People have feared, and at the same time worshiped, natural phenomena such as storms, floods, and volcanos. Even in today's modern world, we speak about some disasters as "acts of God."

Exercise 3: Does attributing natural phenomena to "acts of God" create any confusion in how we view God? Does it make us more aware of God?

God is jealous. We have already seen that God can experience some of the same emotions that humans can—anger, for example. But jealousy is a surprising emotion for us to contemplate about God.

Exercise 4: Consider the word "jealous" in this context. Is it the same emotion we experience or could it mean something more?

When we think of a jealous human we are put off by the emotion—it seems to indicate insecurity, self-centeredness, or lack of trust in another. But this is not how we usually think about God. Perhaps the "jealousy" indicates that God's desire for us is the best path for our happiness and fulfillment. This perspective makes the most sense in light of the last part of the commandment— "I keep faith with those who love me and keep my commandments." He wants to hold us close, and desires our ultimate good.

Isaiah provides more insight into this commandment than do the verses in Exodus 20. When people bow down to gods, they have created themselves, they ask to be saved by the very god they themselves have created. They don't understand (44:17–18). Jesus expanded this idea to things like money and possessions. The story of the rich young ruler exemplifies this in that the man could not chose God over his riches (Matthew 19:21–22).

Commandment Number Three—**Do Not Misuse God's Name**

"You shall not make wrongful use of the name of the LORD your God, for the LORD will not acquit anyone who misuses His name" (Exodus 20:7).

God desires respect. This is much, much more than using the word "god" as a swear word although those of us who love Him are hurt when we hear that usage. We pray, "Hallowed be thy name." We sing songs of praise about God. This commandment acknowledges the awesome greatness of God. We are not to bring dishonor on God in any way. The commandment notes that anyone who is disrespectful of God will be held accountable.

Exercise 5: Are you ever guilty of flippantly using words about God? Does this commandment include such usages as, "Oh my god?" What about OMG? Does this commandment include misuse of the name of Jesus?

Category Two: The Transition Commandment

Commandment number four seems to be about both God and humans. This transitions into the remaining commandments which teach us how to live righteously.

Commandment Number Four—**Keep a Holy Day**

Remember the sabbath day, and keep it holy. Six days you shall labor and do all your work. But the seventh day is a sabbath to the LORD your God; you shall not do any work—you, your son or your daughter, your male or female slave, your livestock, or the alien resident in your towns. For in six days the LORD made heaven and earth, the sea, and all that is in them, but rested the seventh day; therefore, the LORD blessed the sabbath day and consecrated it (Exodus 20:8–11).

Exercise 6: What can we learn about God from this commandment? Is the day of rest provided for God alone, only for humans, or for both? Is it totally about 'rest' or is it about worship?

John Piper, chancellor of Bethlehem College and Seminary and author of more than 50 books, says about those who have no holy day:

By and large, they seem careless, not thoughtful about what they're doing. And they default to professional sports, and TV, and movies. And you look at it and say, 'Is Sunday different from Saturday? Is there anything special about the calendar day of Sunday?' And there are a lot of Christians who say, "No, there is nothing special about it."[1]

There are some people, of course, who cannot take a specific day of rest. These include hospital workers, utility workers, and the waiters who serve us at our Sunday after-church lunch. Consider that if you do not dine out but eat at home after church, the cook in your family may not get a day of rest. In Genesis, it is suggested that "rest" was the reason God stopped creating. Perhaps, the principle of a day of rest is that God has commanded us to observe a time when we can rejuvenate our minds and bodies. And if we are worshipful people, we will use that day to focus on God.

There have been those so committed to honoring God's commandments that they refused to fight in a war on the Sabbath (the Maccabees, 166-164 BCE) thereby choosing death rather than to dishonor the Sabbath.

Exercise 7: Is there a commandment so important to you that you would die rather than disobey? Is it this one?

God cares about all of creation. Note that we are to provide rest for our animals one day each week. This may have been more meaningful in ancient times when animals were used to pull cultivating tools such as plows, and to provide transportation for humans. But in today's world we have horses that pull tourists around historical cities every day of the week.

Exercise 8: How do you observe "the Lord's day?" Ever mow the lawn on Sunday afternoon? What is your "holy time?"

Category Three: Rules for Righteous Living

The following commandments are directed at how humans should treat each other.

Commandment Number Five— Honor Parents

"Honor your father and your mother, so that your days may be long in the land that the Lord your God is giving you" (Exodus 20:12).

God rewards obedience. This commandment promises long life if we obey it, making it both something to obey and a reward for obeying. Throughout the Bible there are statements about parents and the obedience children owe them—Ephesians 6:1, Romans 1:30, Jeremiah 35:18–19, and Matthew 15:3–9. Even Jesus—the Son of God, obeyed his earthly parents (Luke 2:51).

God teaches us to live better. What does it mean "to honor" parents? In ancient nomadic times, maintaining the elderly in a tribe was difficult as the group moved around from one grazing land and oasis to another. It was much easier to simply drop the elderly person by the road side to survive or not, thereby divesting the mobile tribe of the burden of frail members. Jared Diamond's research into modern nomadic culture found that even today, "traditional nomadic tribes often end up abandoning their elderly during their unrelenting travels."[2] Therefore, the commandment given to the Hebrews to honor parents shows how God led the covenant people to become more compassionate.

Exercise 9: How is this ancient custom different from putting our elders in nursing homes and never visiting them? Sometimes parents or grandparents need nursing care, but how should we behave towards them while they are confined?

Exercise 10: What about the behavior of Jesus? Luke 14:26 speaks of "hating" one's family if the goal was to follow Jesus. How do you explain this?

God cares about all of us. Obedience is how young children honor their parents. Adult children honor parents by treating them with respect, by listening to their life stories and advice, and by caring for their needs as they age. This commandment lets us know to value those older and with more life experience than we might have, even when they become frail and weak. What may seem like a burden to young adults will become a great blessing as promised in this commandment.

Jesus countered a question from the Pharisees about his lack of respect for traditions with, "Why do you break God's commandment in the interest of your tradition? For God said, 'Honor your father and mother', and, 'The man who curses his father or mother must suffer death'" (Matthew 15:3–4). We learn from this passage that "to honor" means more than lip service, but must include actions as well.

Exercise 11: How do you go about honoring other authorities such as those in government, police, and employers?

God wants us to rely on him. These ten commandments were never meant to be all inclusive. If they were, then Leviticus and other books would not be filled with further instructions from God. "The Bible is written for a broad population of God's children, and some individuals within that population will have unique situations to which broad teachings cannot necessarily be applied. Not everything in the Bible is written for a particular circumstance."[3] The take-away message is that God knows us as individuals, and responds to us as individuals.

Exercise 12: How does this commandment apply to parents who are abusive to their children?

The fifth commandment was not written as a directive to honor abusive parents, but it is rather a broad principle for living. For instance, while the New Testament writer of 1 Timothy 5:17 provides instructions for us to honor our religious leaders, Jesus did not give honor to those religious leaders who were abusing their powers; he called them "whited sepulchers" (Matthew 23:27). Another example of when Jesus disobeyed a commandment is when he was accused of dishonoring the sabbath rules in order to heal the sick.

This commandment should be approached from at least two perspectives, that of the dependent child and of the adult. As Christians, we try to be aware of children in desperate situations, and to step in with whatever assistance we have. This may include legal and psychological help for the young ones. Adults with a past history of being abused can be helped to forgive, to know it was not their fault, and to recognize mental illness even in their own parents. Adults are not free to abuse those who abused them when they were small and weak. Adults honor abusive parents by helping them to heal, by forgiving them, and by showing love even with a difficult history between them.

There are parents who maintain an abusive relationship with grown children. These parents may interfere in marriages, steal money, or manipulate in harmful ways. If no amount of love can change these people, honoring them may mean "letting your abusers live their lives in peace and be who they are, while you live yours in peace on the other side of the country."[3]

The commandment does not say, "only honor great parents." This is because no one is perfect, and the best parents will make mistakes. We are to do our best to notice the good things parents do for us, to obey their good teachings, and to care for them when it is our turn to be the adults.[4]

Exercise 13: Does this commandment only refer to the egg and sperm donor responsible for one's life?

Commandment Number Six—**No Murder**

"You shall not murder" (Exodus 20:13).

<u>**God values life**</u>. This commandment is just plain logical; of course, no one should take the life of another! With just a little thought, however, one can question the specifics of this rule.

Exercise 14: What about war? What about defending our families, or one's own life? What about capital punishment? If you have opinions about these questions please discuss in light of the sixth commandment, and be kind with each other as you discuss.

On the one hand—OK to kill in war: Christian leaders have historically provided reasons to reject total obedience to this commandment. Martin Luther taught the idea of the "just war. There have been two Popes, Paul VI and John Paul II, who called pacifism "a cowardly and lazy conception of life."[5] Reinhold Niebuhr wrote in support of taking life in some instances in his thesis *Why the Christian Church is not Pacifist.*[5] R. H. Bainton's work in *Christian Attitudes toward War and Peace* details the journey from the very early church's belief in pacifism changing to just war and finally to a belief in holy war.[6] These arguments provide us with reasons for what we do as nations in regard to the taking of life—we may kill in war or capital punishment, but not consider that as being murder.

Biblical arguments for allowing the taking of human life can be found throughout the Old Testament. Deuteronomy 20 is all about how to conduct war against enemies. Exodus 21:24 justifies a life for a life, and an eye for an eye. There are many instances in the Old Testament where the Hebrews kill—the rulers (Egyptians) or the occupants of a land (Amalekites, Midianites, Jericho). Other passages include 1 Samuel 11, Judges 6-7, Joshua 20.

On the other hand—No killing at all: The other side of this discussion is also represented in the Bible. We have the example Jesus provided. When Peter cut the ear of Malchus in the Garden of Gethsemane, Jesus healed the ear and berated the disciple (Luke 47:49–51). Jesus said to turn the other cheek when we are struck. Jesus did not protest his own death even though his "crimes" were merely challenging the religious rulers and traditions of the time.

War seems to present the biggest problem since so many soldiers and innocents can be killed. Many of the early church leaders argued against Christians becoming soldiers or anyone participating in war. "Roland Bainton in *Christian Attitudes Toward War and Peace* stated, 'All of the outstanding writers of the east and of the west repudiated participation in warfare for Christians.' This position has also been argued by Cadoux in *The Early Christian Attitude to War.*"[7] Tertullian, an early church leader, taught against war and in favor of efforts to relieve human suffering. But his efforts had a great deal to do with the way soldiers behaved while at war rather than the idea of war itself.[7] The position of the General Conference of Mennonite Churches wrote in 1953: "We believe that war is altogether contrary to the teaching and spirit of Christ and the Gospel; that therefore war is sin."[8]

Exercise 15: In war, killing is done in the heat of battle; in capital punishment, the taking of a life is deliberate and done in a cold, state-sanctioned manner. What does the group think about this distinction?

Another perspective: When something <u>must</u> be done, pacifists make a distinction between inaction versus active nonviolence. Gandhi believed in nonviolent resistance, and expressed contempt for those who did nothing in the name of pacifism. Gandhi's active nonviolence led to the British partitioning of India. However, one can only wonder what the active nonviolent pacifist would have done to save the six million Jews from Hitler's killing machine.

<u>**God wants us to tame our baser emotions**</u>. Perhaps the answer is an even stricter control of our emotions and actions. "You have heard that it was said to those of old, 'You shall not murder; and whoever murders will be liable to judgment.' But I say to you that everyone who is angry with his brother will be liable to judgment" (Matthew 5:21–22).

Commandment Number Seven—No Adultery

"You shall not commit adultery" (Exodus 20:14).

Exercise 16: What is your definition of adultery? Is it only when one or both parties are married? Do you make a further distinction? Can actions of sexual harassment come under this commandment?

In ancient times, adultery was seen as a crime against the husband of the woman involved. It was a polygamous time (examples of Isaac, Jacob), but men still wanted to know that the children they supported were their own. Therefore, this was primarily a commandment for women to follow, and could result in stoning of the woman.

Jesus told us that even lust in one's heart was sinful. Simply ogling a woman meant adultery had been committed. In modern times we behave in a bimodal manner. We hold many people accountable for adultery, but seem to be forgiving of celebrities.

In Western society, we may frown at adultery in our neighbor, but we no longer stone anyone. This is not true of some cultures even today where stoning involves the crowd throwing a few rocks followed by a truck filled with stones dumping the load on the individual. Jesus stopped stoning from happening once when he asked the crowd if anyone among them was sinless.

Exercise 17: "Let anyone among you who is without sin be the first to throw a stone at her" (John 8:7). How can we apply this wisdom in our own lives? Discuss how these words from Jesus may apply to commandment seven.

Commandment Number Eight—No Stealing

"You shall not steal" (Exodus 20:15).

Jewish scholars indicate that "stealing" also included kidnapping—the stealing of a person or trafficking in human slavery. Modern individuals recognize the need to have laws against stealing, and against kidnapping. As with most things having to do with obedience to God, there are questions we have about something that really should be as straightforward as "Don't take things that aren't yours!"

Exercise 18: What if my family is hungry and I have no money? What if I am a spy and am stealing secrets from an enemy? Is it wrong for the U.S. to try to steal information from North Korea, for example? What are the limits to this commandment, if any?

Exercise 19: Is it OK to purchase something you know is worth a lot more than the person is asking for it without giving the fair amount? If someone is desperate for money but is willing to work for it, is it OK to give that person lower wages than the market requires? Is inequality in pay between the sexes the same as stealing?

Commandment Number Nine—No Untruths

"You shall not bear false witness against your neighbor" (Exodus 20:16).

This commandment poses a conundrum for those among us who are literalists. It says not to lie about neighbors. It does not say never to lie. So, what can we determine about God from this? Is it that God wants us to be truthful about other people? Or does God want us to be truthful in all things?

Again, we have a commandment that seems to be very clear—don't lie about your neighbor. Lying imposes heavy emotions of guilt and shame for the inexperienced liar, and can become so common place for the experienced liar that truth and lies become indistinguishable. John 8:32 tells us that truth will free us. The rest of this passage says that committing sin condemns us to be slaves to that sin. Common sense tells us that a lie will require care and feeding for as long as the lie is to be maintained; it cannot be ignored without exposing the liar. This can become a heavy burden, making us become slaves to the lie.

Passages that speak to us of truth especially concerning Jesus include: "And the Word became flesh and lived among us, and we have seen his glory, the glory as of a father's only son, full of grace and truth" (John 1:14), and "The law indeed was given through Moses; grace and truth came through Jesus Christ" (John 1:17). We even equate Jesus with truth: "I am the Way, the Truth, and the Life" (John 14:6).

Exercise 20: Did the family that hid Anne Frank and her family from the Nazis break this commandment by lying to the Gestapo?

Exercise 21: Have you ever lied to spare someone's feelings? For example, when asked if the new dress, "makes me look fat" what is your first reaction?

God wants us to be just in the treatment of others. Perhaps this commandment is connected more to the remainder of the sentence: "against thy neighbor." This raises the question asked in the Good Samaritan parable: Who is my neighbor? How far away from us and our neighborhood does this commandment extend?

THE FOURTH CATEGORY INVOLVES ONLY ONE PERSON

The final commandment does not tell us how to worship God, nor does it tell us how to live in harmony with other humans. It is about who we are as individuals. It asks us to look inside ourselves and be generous of spirit.

Category Four: A Rule for the Inner Person

Commandment Number Ten—**Do Not Covet Anything of Another's**

"You shall not covet your neighbor's house; you shall not covet your neighbor's wife, or male or female slave, or ox, or donkey, or anything that belongs to your neighbor" (Exodus 20:17).

God desires faithfulness in our thoughts and actions. Here we have an example of a sin that is of the mind or the imagination, just like lust. If you desire to have something that already belongs to another, that is a wrong-headed thing. This commandment does not say, "Thou shalt not steal your neighbor's possessions…" It says to not <u>desire</u> something belonging to another.

The Commandments are a list of actions and thoughts to guide our worship (have no other gods), and our ethics (don't steal). The Old Testament is filled with things to do and not to do—these 10 stand out. This final commandment is different from the other nine in that it addresses the inner person—don't desire what others have.

Jesus told us that our thoughts are important, and sometimes as bad as actually taking action (Matthew 5:28). Perhaps thoughts lead to resentment of God for not giving some coveted item to us instead of to another person. Discontent with one's own life, or desire for what another has can lead to unhappiness, to stealing, to harm of others. It is not "things" that should occupy our desires, but service for God; placing love of things above God is idolatry. Jesus said that a full life did not depend on possessions (Luke 12:15). James goes on to describe how covetous desire leads to evil deeds (James 1:14–15).

Exercise 22: Have you had the experience of being jealous of a sibling or a co-worker for what he or she has?

CONCLUSION

God gave us the ten commandments as broad principles governing worship of God, relationships with others, and personal growth. Jesus gave the ten commandments a fresh approach when he said that even anger would make us open to judgment (Matthew 5:21–22). Jesus holds us to a higher standard than just refusing to act on our desires. We are to maintain pure hearts and thoughts, and to find satisfaction in the blessings God has given us. We are to love our neighbor as ourselves, to forsake love of money, to forgive the son who breaks his parent's heart, and to love only God. These are first things of the heart, soul, and mind which can be translated into righteous actions.

We came into the world naked and totally dependent. We will take nothing from the world except when God says, "Good and faithful Servant!"

REFERENCES

1. Piper, J. (2008, December). *What does it mean practically to keep the Sabbath holy?* Retrieved from http://www.desiringgod.org/interviews/what-does-it-mean-practically-to-keep-the-sabbath-holy.
2. Lin, J. (2010, January 7). Honor or abandon: Societies' treatment of elderly intrigues scholar. *UCLA Newsroom.* Retrieved from http://newsroom.ucla.edu/stories/jared-diamond-on-aging-150571
3. Pittelli, R. (2002). *Is God really telling us to honor abusive parents?* Retrieved from http://www.luke173ministries.org/537996.
4. Ortberg, N. (2006). *Honor thy father and mother?* Retrieved from http://www.todayschristianwoman.com/articles/2006/may/4.38.html.
5. Grimsrud, T. (n.d.). *Peace theology: Engaging peace and pacifism.* Retrieved from https://peacetheology.net/pacifism/1-introduction-defining-pacifism/

6   Bainton, R.H. (1979). *Christian attitudes toward war and peace: A historical survey and critical re-evaluation*. Eugene, Oregon: Wipf and Stock.
7   Morey, R. (2009). *The early church, war and pacifism*. Retrieved from http://www.churchinhistory.org/pages/misc/ch-war-pac.htm.
8   General Conference Mennonite Church (1953). *A Christian declaration on peace, war, and military service*, (adopted at Portland, Oregon, August 22, 1953.) Retrieved from http://home.mennonitechurch.ca/1953-declarationonpeace, p.1.

CHAPTER 10   LEADER'S GUIDE: THE COMMANDMENTS
EXODUS 20

PRELIMINARY THOUGHTS

There are ten sections in this discussion of the ten commandments. The commandments themselves are often very different so the topics will change considerably between each section. It will be the leader's job to keep the group focused on what each commandment tells us about God.

Exercise 1: How many of the ten commandants can the class can remember?

You might write these on a board, and revisit at the end of the lesson to see if more are remembered then. Or you may want to discuss why specific ones were not remembered. Emphasize that while we have many other "laws" of righteous living to remember from the Bible, Jesus really simplified things for us by stating the two greatest commandments.

THE FOUR CATEGORIES OF COMMANDMENTS

The commandment discussions are organized into four categories in order to emphasize the relationship among them, and how they address the important aspects of our lives.

Category One: The Place of God in Our Lives

Commandment Number One—**No Other Gods**

Exercise 2: What "gods" do we have before us today? Are you in danger of letting something take first place in your life over God such as social position or patriotism? Or perhaps you place your family above all else? Has this commandment meant something special to you personally?

Examples may include money, power, patriotism, lust. Or maybe self-esteem is so low that worship of personal trappings satisfies a desperate feeling of unworthiness.

Commandment Number Two—**No Images to Worship**

Exercise 3: Does attributing natural phenomena to "acts of God" create any confusion in how we view God? Does it make us more aware of God?

Does this allow us to "blame" God for weather disasters? Address the fact that one TV evangelist said Hurricane Katrina devastated New Orleans because it was a sinful city. That same individual had no blame to place about Hurricane Harvey in Texas, a state generally seen to be predominantly Christian. Tread gently with this topic because many people love TV evangelists, and some are worthy to be honored—Rev. Billy Graham, an exemplary Christian, was not strictly a "TV evangelist" but used television to reach the masses with the message of salvation. Try to get them to think about whether God is actively causing everything, or if He set nature in motion and allows it to play out.

Exercise 4: Consider the word "jealous" in this context. Is it the same emotion we experience or could it mean something more?

God is jealous FOR us in that His desire for creation is that we make the best choices for happiness and righteousness. The commandment includes the assurance that He keeps faith with us.

Commandment Number Three—**Do Not Misuse God's Name**

> "A.W. Tozer in his classic book on the attributes of God, *The Knowledge of the Holy* says, 'Why would he make such an extreme pronouncement?' Tozer goes on to say, 'Man's spiritual history will positively demonstrate that no religion has ever been greater than its idea of God. Worship is pure or base as the worshipper entertains high or low thoughts of God.'"[1]

Let the group consider what it would mean for the worship of God if we were allowed to use His name in any way we wanted. Some people already seem to do this.

Exercise 5: Are you ever guilty of flippantly using words about God? Does this commandment include such usages as, "Oh my god?" What about OMG? Does this commandment include the name of Jesus?

Perhaps the difference between disrespect and common language usage lies in the use of the word God versus god. There are many gods—money, power, sex, but only one God.

Category Two: The Transition Commandment

Commandment Number Four—**Keep a Holy Day**

Exercise 6: What can we learn about God from this commandment? Is the day of rest provided for God alone, only for humans, or for both? Is it totally about 'rest' or is it about worship?

Is this commandment something God needs?

Exercise 7: Is there a commandment so important to you that you would die rather than disobey? Is it this one?

Give them time to ponder this. Would they die rather than commit murder? Ask them if they would be able to have the job of executing a convicted criminal? Could they turn off the ventilator when a patient had been declared brain dead? Would they rather die than covet? Than lie? Than…

Probably you will find that an honest group will say none of the commandments are worth dying for. If this is the case, ask the group to consider the importance of this finding. Does God ask us to die to keep his commandments? Perhaps these are rules to help us have happier lives, rather than rules to die for. Remember that God turned the first humans out of the garden for disobeying the only commandment he gave them—not to eat fruit of one tree. God did not kill them for this first disobedience.

Exercise 8: How do you observe "the Lord's day?" Ever mow the lawn on Sunday afternoon? What is your "holy time?"

Let the group discuss. They may offer reasons for work on Sunday such as "I work at my job the rest of the week, and this is the only time I have to mow the lawn." Guide the discussion to see if they feel the lack of rest harms them.

Focus on what we can learn about God _rather than_ on what the class members do on Sundays. After all, they are in your class now rather than lying in bed at home!

Different groups feel strongly about which day of the week we should rest. We will not take sides here since Genesis does not list the day God rested as Friday, Saturday, or Sunday; the calendar we use came much later in history. Many Christian groups—Presbyterian, Congregationalist, Methodist, and Baptists among them, worship on the calendar day of Sunday.

God cares about the animals: Note that we are to provide rest for our animals one day each week. This may have been more meaningful in ancient times when animals were used to pull cultivating tools such as plows, and to provide transportation for humans. But in today's modern world we have horses that pull tourists around historical cities all through the week.

Category Three: Rules for Righteous Living

Commandment Number Five—**Honor Parents**

Exercise 9: How is this ancient custom different from putting our elders in nursing homes and never visiting them? Sometimes parents or grandparents need nursing care, but how should we behave towards them while they are confined?

Start the discussion by asking the group if adults must put aside dreams and ambitions in order to provide care for one or more parents? Ultimately, what would each one regret doing or not having done at the end of life?

Exercise 10: What about the behavior of Jesus? Luke 14:26 speaks of "hating" one's family if the goal was to follow Jesus. How do you explain this?

Set the discussion in the time and culture of Palestine during Jesus' time. The Romans were in charge, and the priestly community benefited from the relationship with Rome. If parents were too frightened of the priests and Romans to follow Jesus, the child should not give consideration to them.

Read the remainder of the story—Luke 14:27–33. Several examples are provided in which something is started but not completed correctly. If we start to build a tower, we must compute the whole cost before beginning to build a tower, or we must prepare for the full cost of war before starting. So, we as followers of Christ must consider the full ramifications before becoming disciples. If parents refuse to believe in Jesus and reject their children, then the children are to turn away from parents and turn toward God. We can interpret this to mean that God is to have our first and fullest devotion.

Other teachings in the New Testament allow us to understand that we do not really "hate," but we can and must turn away from those influences which interfere with devotion to God. See 1 John 4:7–8.

Exercise 11: How do you go about honoring other authorities such as those in government, police, and employers?

Ask them what their parents taught them about respect for authority? How has respect for authority changed since they became adults? How do they teach their children about honoring the elected officials of the "other" party? Is it harmful to the child and to society to teach hatred for any group?

Exercise 12: How does this commandment apply to parents who are abusive to their children?

Have someone read Ezekiel 20:18–19 and Acts 5:29. These verses teach us not to model our lives after ungodly parents, and to obey the heavenly parent first over earthly parents.

Exercise 13: Does this commandment only refer to the egg and sperm donor responsible for one's life?

The obvious answer is "No." We should honor those who have invested their lives in raising us in a loving, caring home environment.

Commandment Number Six—**No Murder**

Exercise 14: What about war? What about defending our families, or one's own life? What about capital punishment? If you have opinions about these questions please discuss in light of the sixth commandment. Be kind with each other as you discuss.

This would be a space where abortion might enter the discussion. Abortion is a topic that many feel very passionate about and the discussion could become heated. Do not introduce the topic of abortion. However, should it arise, the leader should be prepared to play a neutral role while maintaining a courteous approach to the discussion. It may become necessary to move the discussion back to what the lesson is about—learning who God is.

A Personal Word to the Leader: You may have strong, passionate feelings yourself about abortion and you may feel that it is your ethical duty to share your opinion. Try to remember that this curriculum is about discerning as much as we can about the characteristics of God. In addition, this is not the time to engage so strongly that you lose your ability to lead in calm exploration of these issues. Maintaining dialogue about many issues within the safe context of the church is a good and reasonable thing. Maintain the trust of all your class members by not taking either side in this complex matter.

Exercise 15: In war, killing is done in the heat of battle; in capital punishment, the taking of a life is deliberate and done in a cold, state-sanctioned manner. What does the group think about this distinction?

This is another topic that can lead to intense disagreement. Be prepared to guide the discussion in such a way that anyone who wishes to talk is allowed to do so but no one person monopolizes.

Commandment Number Seven—**No Adultery**

Exercise 16: What is your definition of adultery? Is it only when one or both parties are married? Do you make a further distinction? Can actions of sexual harassment come under this commandment?

If adultery is defined as between two people, one or both of whom is married to someone else, this is indeed adultery as we have usually defined it. These actions cause unnecessary hurt to spouses whose trust has been abused, to children who may end up living in split families, and to anyone who may love either of the two people involved in the affair. Discuss who is being hurt or harmed when this adultery occurs. Ask the class to define for themselves what is the sin being perpetrated. Is it unfaithfulness? Betrayal?

Exercise 17: "Let anyone among you who is without sin be the first to throw a stone at her" (John 8:7). How can we apply this wisdom in our own lives? Discuss how these words from Jesus may apply to commandment seven.

Does this mean we are never to condemn anyone for their sins? Are we never to admonish an adult for doing something we consider wrong? We have a judicial system in the United States—does this commandment have anything to do with court findings? Was Jesus just speaking about a very particular occurrence happening in front of him, and we have taken his words to apply universally to our lives? Are we supposed to read Scripture and apply all of it to the living of our lives? Is some of the Bible simply a history?

Commandment Number Eight—**No Stealing**

Exercise 18: What if my family is hungry and I have no money? What if I am a spy and am stealing secrets from an enemy? Is it wrong for the U.S. to try to steal information from North Korea, for example? What are the limits to this commandment, if any?

What if the secrets being stole from an enemy country could lead to war against that country, its soldiers, and its innocent civilians? Focus the group on the characteristic of God that this commandment is exhibiting.

Exercise 19: Is it OK to purchase something you know is worth a lot more than the person is asking for it without giving the fair amount? If someone is desperate for money but is willing to work for it, is it OK to give that person lower wages than the market requires? Is inequality in pay between the sexes for the same work the same as stealing?

If all the world obeyed God's laws, the answers would be no, no, and no. The answers are still probably no, no, and no. Are there circumstances in this imperfect world where any of these three situations are acceptable?

Commandment Number Nine—**No Untruths**

Consider the next two exercises together. Ask if truth is more important than love. It should be obvious that lying is sometimes the better choice. The commandment speaks specifically against telling lies about one's neighbor, probably harmful lies are the intention. What if someone asks me if my neighbor is a good person, and I already have a grievance against that neighbor? Should I put my grievance aside and try to show the neighbor in the best light?

Exercise 20: Did the family that hid Anne Franks and her family from the Nazis break this commandment by lying to the Gestapo?

Exercise 21: Have you ever lied to spare someone's feelings? For example, when asked if the new dress, "makes me look fat" what is your first reaction?

This seems to be a small thing not worth considering; one lies in order to spare someone's feelings. But where does one draw the line? What if the dress really does make the person look bad and the individual is on her way to a job interview? What consequences can result from the small lie?

THE FOURTH CATEGORY INVOLVES ONLY ONE PERSON

Category Four: A Rule for the Inner Person

Commandment Number Ten—**Do Not Covet Anything of Another's**

Exercise 22: Have you had the experience of being jealous of a sibling or a co-worker for what he or she has?

Almost all of us have experienced jealousy at some point. Ask the group to share how they dealt with a jealousy. Discuss what God intended with this commandment.

CONCLUSION

Review the identified characteristics of God in these passages. Does the class agree with these? Are there additions to be listed?

REVISIT THE CENTRAL THEME AND QUESTION.

Central Theme of this Lesson: God gave us instructions on how to live righteous lives.

Central Question of this Lesson: How am I to apply these ancient commandments in modern life?

REFERENCE

1. Tozer, A.W. (1961). *Knowledge of the holy*. Retrieved from http://www.ntcg-aylesbury.org.uk/books/knowledge_of_the_holy.pdf, p.4.

APPENDIX — AUTHOR OF THE FIRST FIVE BOOKS

WHO AND WHEN

The two questions—authorship of the first five books of the Bible, and when were they written—are important questions for those who attempt to seriously study the Bible. The following paragraphs list several of the opinions concerning these questions. Regardless of the origin of these books, the message they contain is illuminating for the purpose of living life. We have been gifted with this "body of knowledge...to enable us to live every moment of our lives with joy and intentionality, in the presence of the true and living God."[1]

Second Timothy 3:15–17 clearly tells us the wonderful things Scripture was intended to do for us—to help us grow into righteousness and to teach us to do good works. But it also lets us know what the Bible was never intended to do. It is not a book of physics, of mathematics, or any of the sciences. Rather than fill in all the answers we could possibly ask about creation, the purpose is to perfect humans morally and spiritually, and to prepare us to do good works.

VIEW NUMBER ONE—MOSES AS AUTHOR

Many people of faith believe that Moses wrote the first five books and base that claim on biblical references. Early references to Moses as author include Exodus 24:4, and Exodus 24:7, AND Exodus 34:27-28.

A New Testament reference to the possible authorship of the Torah is found in Mark 12:26. As Jesus was speaking to some Pharisees and men sent from Herod to trap him, he said the following: "And as for the dead being raised, have you not read in the book of Moses, in the story about the bush, how God said to him, 'I am the God of Abraham, the God of Isaac, and the God of Jacob"? Recently reported archaeological evidence that some biblical texts were in written form in the 10th century BCE means that the rabbis of Jesus' time could have had access to copies.

Professor Gershon Galil of the department of biblical studies at the University of Haifa has deciphered an inscription dating from the 10th century BCE (the period of King David's reign) and has shown it to be a Hebrew inscription. The discovery makes this the earliest known Hebrew writing. The significance of this breakthrough relates to the fact that at least some of the biblical scriptures were composed hundreds of years before the dates presented today in scholarly research.[2]

Other references to Moses as the author are found throughout the Bible. Joshua 8:31–32 speaks of commandments being "written in the book of the law of Moses." Joshua 23:6 refers to "the book of the law of Moses." Other references can be found in Daniel 9:11, and 9:13; Ezra 3:2 and 7:6, Nehemiah 8:1, II Chronicles 23:18 and 30:16. As the reader considers these things, remember that the Bible is not one big book by one writer, but rather numerous manuscripts pulled together into a sacred canon. Churches and people of faith gradually and over hundreds of years decided on which manuscripts were inspired and worthy of being accepted as God's word. The Old Testament books were written originally in Hebrew except for some parts of Daniel (Aramaic). The texts were written between 1200 to 100 BCE and were completed during the period of Achaemenid rule in the 400s BCE.[3] The canon of Scripture we know today first came out of the 393 CE Synod of Hippo. The list was later upheld in 419 at the Council of Carthage. It was at the Council of Trent in 1546 that the canon became official.[4]

Why is this important in a discussion of who wrote the first five books? Because references to Moses as the author are found not just by one writer, but rather found throughout the collected writings of many prophets who gave testimony to his authorship. Just as the testimony of many witnesses in a courtroom adds to the weight of the evidence, so do references by many authors.

VIEW NUMBER TWO—PRIESTLY AUTHOR(S)

There are some problems with the idea that Moses wrote the entire first five books of the First Testament. (1) The verses in Exodus 34 tell us that Moses wrote down something God told him during forty days and nights. But it also notes only two stone tablets were used—hardly enough to cover the entire five books of the Torah. (2) The two tablets were written by the finger of God, not by Moses (Exodus 31:18).

The final reason to believe Moses was not the author is that the death of Moses is recorded in the Torah, making it seem unlikely that Moses himself was the author (Deuteronomy 33:1 and 34:1–12). Argument has been made that the news of Moses' death could have been an insertion by others into the works of the original author; this gives rise to the possibility that many insertions could have been made as well by other scribes and prophets.

In the Mark's Gospel reference above, it is not known if Jesus meant that Moses wrote the Torah, or if he is referring to a book named "the *Book of Moses*." We know that books such as the *Book of Gad* and the *Book of Nathan* (I Chronicles 29:29) have been lost to modern readers as the *Book of Moses* may have been lost. Jesus, raised as the son of a carpenter in Nazareth, most probably did not possess a copy of the scrolls of the Torah, but rather learned Scripture from his boyhood worship experiences with a rabbi. Traditionally, the rabbis would read from a Torah written in Hebrew on a parchment scroll. Regular public reading of the Torah was started during the time of Ezra after the Babylonian captivity was over (c. 537 BCE), as described in the Nehemiah 8. This reading to the congregation would take place publicly at a prescribed time. We are told In Luke 2:46–47 that Jesus knew enough even as a boy to discuss with the Jerusalem rabbis when his parents took him there.

Rabbinical teachings at that time were largely from sacred oral history. The Torah originated from oral tradition according to most modern biblical scholars and took many centuries to be put into written form. This hypothesis is known as the *Documentary Hypothesis* [5] and states that the first and most comprehensive manuscript of the first five books to that point was composed in the late seventh or the sixth century BCE (the Jahwist source). According to this hypothesis, the Torah was later expanded (the Priestly source) into what is very likely the first five books we have today.

What are these sources? There are four hypothesized written sources of the Torah which together form the first five books of the Bible. These four sources are commonly referred to with letters as in J for the Jahwist source, E for Elohist source, P for Priestly source, and D for Deuteronomist source.[5] "The consensus of scholarship is that the stories are taken from four different written sources and that these were brought together over the course of time to form the first five books of the Bible as a composite work."[6] The majority of Biblical scholars posit that committing the Torah to writing from oral tradition and from earlier written sources occurred during the Babylonian captivity around 600 BCE.

Regardless of whether you believe Moses was the author or other priests and scribes wrote the Torah, the scriptures we are blessed to have guide us in how to live, inspire us to reach toward God, and provide hope as we navigate through life's journey.

REFERENCES

1. George, T. (2005). Foreword. In Fisher Humphries', *I Have Called You Friends* Birmingham, AL: New Hope Publishers, p.13.
2. University of Haifa. (2010 January 7). *Most ancient Hebrew biblical inscription deciphered.* Haifa, Israel: University of Haifa. Retrieved from https://www.eurekalert.org/pub_releases/2010-01/uoh-mah010710.php.
3. Editors. (2017). Hebrew Bible: Jewish sacred writings. *Encyclopaedia Britannica.* Retrieved from https://www.britannica.com/topic/Hebrew-Bible.
4. Kelly, J. (n.d.). When was the Bible first written/compiled and by whom? *Quora.* Retrieved from https://www.quora.com/When-was-the-Bible-first-written-compiled-and-by-whom.
5. _____. (n.d.). Student zone: Religious texts biblical criticism source criticism. *The Tablet.* Retrieved from https://www.thetablet.co.uk/student-zone/religious-texts/biblical-criticism/source-criticism.

6. Riches, J. (2000). *The Bible: A very short introduction*. Oxford: Oxford University Press. pp. 19–20. Retrieved from https://en.wikipedia.org/wiki/Torah.

www.ingramcontent.com/pod-product-compliance
Lightning Source LLC
Chambersburg PA
CBHW081722100526

44591CB00016B/2465